Houghton Mifflin

Math Expressions

Volume 1

Homework and Remembering

Developed by
The Children's Math Worlds
Research Project

PROJECT DIRECTOR AND AUTHOR

Dr. Karen C. Fuson

This material is based upon work supported by the
National Science Foundation
under Grant Numbers
ESI-9816320, REC-9806020, and RED-935373.

Any opinions, findings, and conclusions or recommendations expressed in this material are those of the author and do not necessarily reflect the views of the National Science Foundation.

HOUGHTON MIFFLIN BOSTON

Teacher Reviewers

Kindergarten
Patricia Stroh Sugiyama
Wilmette, Illinois

Barbara Wahle
Evanston, Illinois

Grade 1
Sandra Budson
Newton, Massachusetts

Janet Pecci
Chicago, Illinois

Megan Rees
Chicago, Illinois

Grade 2
Molly Dunn
Danvers, Massachusetts

Agnes Lesnick
Hillside, Illinois

Rita Soto
Chicago, Illinois

Grade 3
Jane Curran
Honesdale, Pennsylvania

Sandra Tucker
Chicago, Illinois

Grade 4
Sara Stoneberg Llibre
Chicago, Illinois

Sheri Roedel
Chicago, Illinois

Grade 5
Todd Atler
Chicago, Illinois

Leah Barry
Norfolk, Massachusetts

Credits

Cover art: (tiger) © Juniors Bildarchiv/Alamy Images. (whale) © Francois Gohier/Photo Researchers, Inc. (grass) © Corel Stock Photo Library. (tape) © Eyewire.

Illustrative art: Robin Boyer/Deborah Wolfe, LTD
Technical art: Nesbitt Graphics, Inc.
Photos: Nesbitt Graphics, Inc.

Printed in the U.S.A.

ISBN-13: 978-0-618-64112-3
ISBN-10: 0-618-64112-2

9 1421 11
4500331386

1–1

Homework

Name ______________________

Solve the story problems. | **Show your work.**

1. Spencer saw 8 frogs in the pond. Then he saw 5 more. How many frogs did Spencer see altogether?

☐ ______________
label

frog

2. Beth has 5 red marbles and some blue marbles. Altogether she has 14 marbles. How many of the marbles are blue?

☐ ______________
label

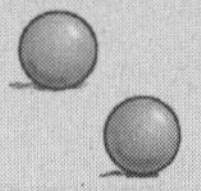
marbles

3. Felix has 5 stamps from Mexico. The rest are from Canada. He has 8 stamps altogether. How many stamps are from Canada?

☐ ______________
label

stamp

4. Gary had 7 books. His mother gave him 3 more books. How many books does Gary have now?

☐ ______________
label

book

5. On the Back Write your own story problem. Then show how to solve it.

Name

Name ____________________

Homework

Solve the story problems.

Show your work.

1. There were 15 lights on. Then some of the lights burned out. Now there are 6 lights on. How many lights burned out?

light

☐ ____________________
label

2. Kari scored 7 points at soccer practice. Shona scored 3. How many more points did Kari score than Shona?

soccer ball

☐ ____________________
label

3. There are 4 screwdrivers and some hammers in a toolbox. Altogether there are 9 tools. How many hammers are there?

tools

☐ ____________________
label

4. Obi picked 14 cucumbers. Pam picked 8. How many more cucumbers would Pam have to pick to have as many as Obi?

cucumber

☐ ____________________
label

5. Show a Proof Drawing Choose one of the problems on this page. Show a Proof Drawing for the problem.

1–2 Name ____________________

Remembering

Solve the story problems. | **Show your work.**

1. Andy has 9 toys. Andy gave Yori 4 toys. How many toys does Andy have left?

☐ ____________________
label

toy

2. Tracy has 7 green marbles and some yellow marbles. Altogether she has 10 marbles. How many of them are yellow?

☐ ____________________
label

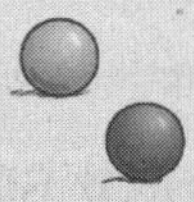

marbles

3. Imala has 5 balls. John has 2. How many balls do they have altogether?

☐ ____________________
label

ball

4. There are 3 boys and some girls on the train. There are 7 children on the train. How many girls are on the train?

☐ ____________________
label

train

5. Explain Your Thinking On a separate piece of paper, explain all the steps you took to solve problem 4.

1–3

Homework

Name ______________________________

Add or subtract.

1. 7 + 1 = ☐	5 − 0 = ☐	0 + 1 = ☐
2. 3 + 0 = ☐	9 − 1 = ☐	6 + 1 = ☐
3. 0 + 7 = ☐	2 − 0 = ☐	4 + 1 = ☐
4. 4 + 1 = ☐	3 − 1 = ☐	6 + 0 = ☐
5. 9 + 0 = ☐	5 − 1 = ☐	9 + 1 = ☐
6. 1 + 8 = ☐	2 − 1 = ☐	10 − 0 = ☐
7. 1 + 3 = ☐	4 − 0 = ☐	8 − 0 = ☐
8. 0 + 5 = ☐	6 − 0 = ☐	3 + 1 = ☐
9. 5 + 1 = ☐	7 − 1 = ☐	6 − 1 = ☐
10. 0 + 4 = ☐	8 − 0 = ☐	1 − 1 = ☐

11. **On the Back** What happens when you add 0 to a number? Draw a picture to explain.

Name

Name ______________________

Homework

Solve the story problems.

Show your work.

1. There were 12 clean glasses in the dish rack. Matt put some of them away. Now there are 5 glasses left in the rack. How many glasses did Matt put away?

glasses

☐ ______________________
label

2. There are 2 flowers in a red vase and some flowers in a white vase. There are 8 flowers altogether. How many flowers are in the white vase?

flowers

☐ ______________________
label

3. Carlos took 10 pictures with his camera. Jane took 6 pictures. How many more pictures must Jane take in order to have as many as Carlos?

camera

☐ ______________________
label

4. Jung Mee has 9 tomatoes growing in her garden. She has 8 tomatoes in the kitchen. How many tomatoes does Jung Mee have in total?

tomato

☐ ______________________
label

 Name ______________________

Remembering

Solve the story problems. | **Show your work.**

1. Mary spent $3 at the toy store. Jamal spent $6 more than Mary. How many dollars did Jamal spend at the toy store?

toy

☐ ______________
label

2. Aaron bought 5 hats at the store. Lucia bought 8 hats. How many more hats must Aaron buy to have as many as Lucia?

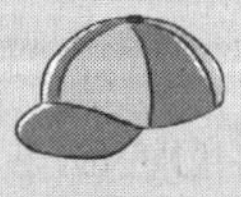
hat

☐ ______________
label

Add or subtract 0 or 1.

3. 4 + 1 = ☐	9 − 1 = ☐	0 + 7 = ☐
4. 9 + 1 = ☐	6 − 0 = ☐	2 + 0 = ☐
5. 1 + 3 = ☐	6 − 1 = ☐	9 + 0 = ☐
6. 0 + 5 = ☐	8 − 0 = ☐	6 + 1 = ☐
7. 7 + 1 = ☐	7 − 1 = ☐	1 + 5 = ☐
8. 0 + 4 = ☐	1 − 1 = ☐	1 + 8 = ☐

1–5

Name ____________________

Homework

1. What teen numbers are shown here?

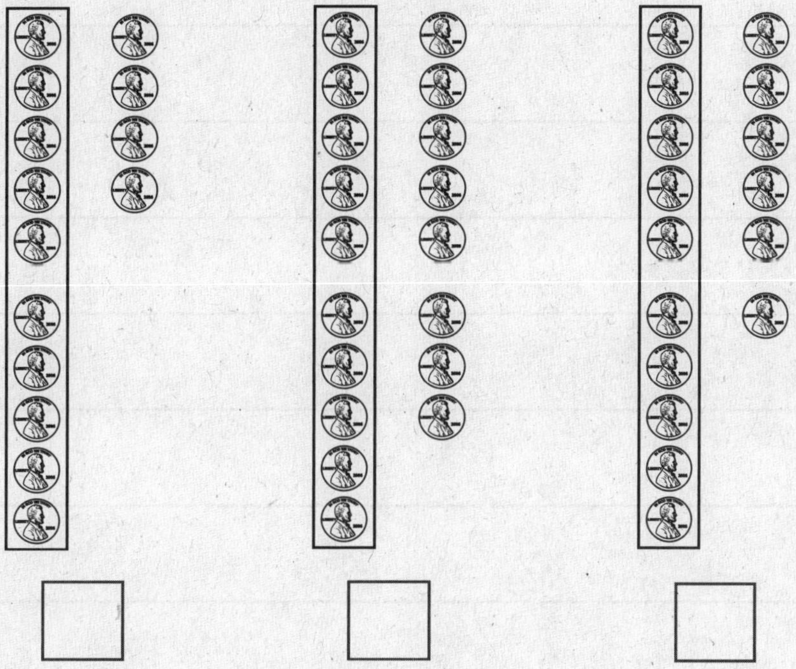

10 + 6 = ____

10 + 2 = ____

10 + 4 = ____

10 + 1 = ____

10 + 3 = ____

10 + 5 = ____

10 + 8 = ____

10 + 7 = ____

10 + 9 = ____

2. Ring the pennies needed to make each teen number.

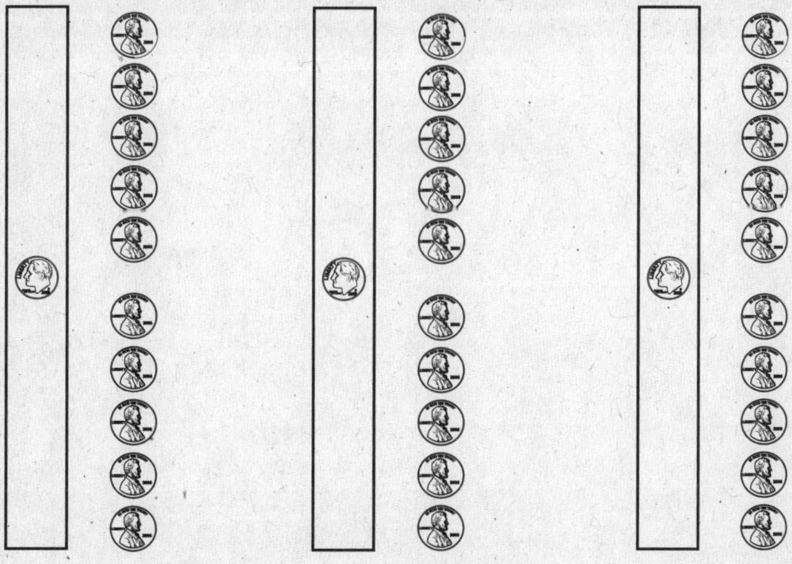

17 12 15

12 = 10 + ____

16 = 10 + ____

18 = 10 + ____

11 = 10 + ____

17 = 10 + ____

14 = 10 + ____

13 = 10 + ____

15 = 10 + ____

19 = 10 + ____

3. On the Back Write and solve a story problem about pennies.

Name

1–6 Name ____________________

Homework

Count the rabbits in the garden. Then write the partners of 10.

1.

10 = ___ + ___

10 = ___ + ___

10 = ___ + ___

2.

10 = ___ + ___

10 = ___ + ___

10 = ___ + ___

3.

10 = ___ + ___

10 = ___ + ___

10 = ___ + ___

---

4. Write the partners of 10 that are the same but are switched.

1 + 9 = 9 + 1

___ + ___ = ___ + ___

___ + ___ = ___ + ___

___ + ___ = ___ + ___

1–6 Name ______________________

Remembering

Solve the story problems. | **Show your work.**

1. Sally had 9 tomatoes. She and her friends ate 4. How many tomatoes are left?

☐ ______________________
label

tomato

2. On Jerome's desk, 6 folders are open. The rest are closed. There are 9 folders on Jerome's desk. How many folders on his desk are closed?

☐ ______________________
label

folder

What teen numbers are shown here?

3.

☐

☐

☐

19 = 10 + ____

12 = 10 + ____

14 = 10 + ____

18 = 10 + ____

11 = 10 + ____

15 = 10 + ____

17 = 10 + ____

13 = 10 + ____

16 = 10 + ____

1–7 Name ______

Homework

Write the number partners and the total for the picture.

1. 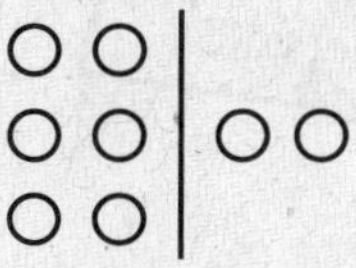

Number Partners

____ and ____

Total ______

2. 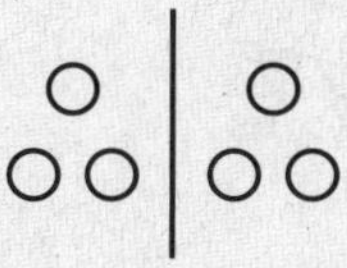

Number Partners

____ and ____

Total ______

3. 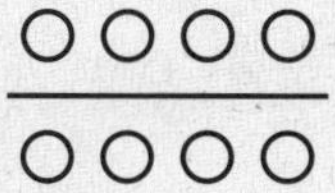

Number Partners

____ and ____

Total ______

4. 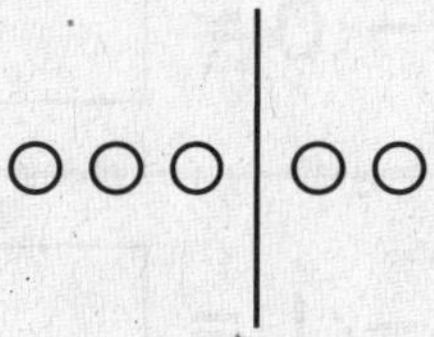

Number Partners

____ and ____

Total ______

5. 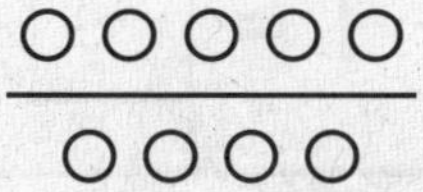

Number Partners

____ and ____

Total ______

6. 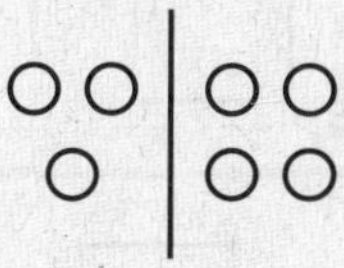

Number Partners

____ and ____

Total ______

7. Create Your Own Draw your own picture.
Write the number partners and total for your picture.

Number Partners

____ and ____

Total ______

1–7 Name

Targeted Practice

Watch the signs!

Add or subtract.

1. 4 + 1 = ☐	1 − 1 = ☐	5 − 1 = ☐
2. 6 + 1 = ☐	8 − 0 = ☐	3 − 1 = ☐
3. 0 + 1 = ☐	8 − 1 = ☐	2 − 0 = ☐
4. 0 + 10 = ☐	1 − 0 = ☐	9 − 1 = ☐
5. 8 + 1 = ☐	4 − 1 = ☐	5 − 0 = ☐
6. 1 + 0 = ☐	10 − 1 = ☐	7 − 0 = ☐
7. 5 + 1 = ☐	9 − 0 = ☐	1 + 7 = ☐
8. 6 + 0 = ☐	10 − 0 = ☐	9 + 0 = ☐

9. **Critical Thinking** How are adding 0 and subtracting 0 the same?

____

____

1–8

Homework

Name ____________________

Complete the Partner Houses.

1.

8	
+	+
+	+
+	+
+	

2	
+	

5	
+	+
+	+

2.

3	
+	+

6	
+	+
+	+
+	

10	
+	+
+	+
+	+
+	+
+	

3.

7	
+	+
+	+
+	+

9	
+	+
+	+
+	+
+	+

4	
+	+
+	

4. Which Partner Houses have doubles?

Name ______________________________

Remembering

Count the rabbits in the garden. Then write the partners of 10. Then switch the partners.

1.

10 = ___ + ___

10 = ___ + ___

2.

10 = ___ + ___

10 = ___ + ___

3.

10 = ___ + ___

10 = ___ + ___

What teen numbers are shown here?

4.

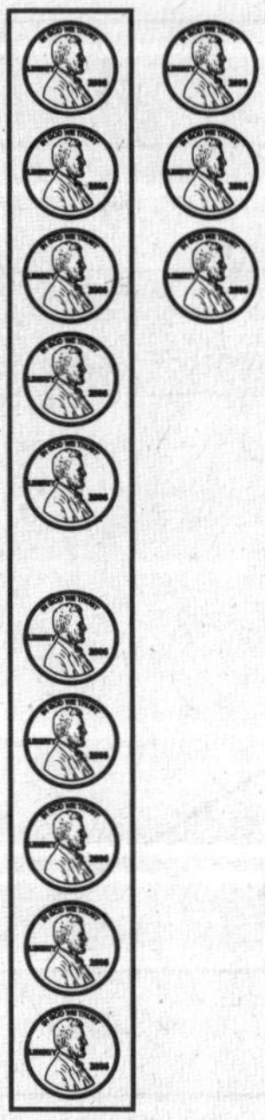

☐

5.

☐

6.

☐

7.

☐

Name ____________________

Homework

6 + 3 = [9]

6 Already 6 | 7 8 9

I pretend I already counted 6. So **6**, 7, 8, 9.

Already **6** 7 8 9

Already **6** 7 8 9

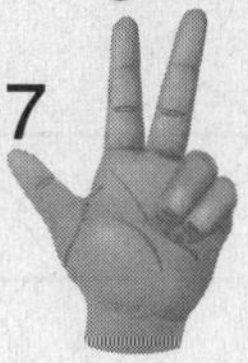

Count on to find the total.

1. 5 + 4 = ☐ 4 + 7 = ☐ 7 + 2 = ☐

2. 4 + 3 = ☐ 2 + 6 = ☐ 5 + 2 = ☐

3. 7 + 5 = ☐ 5 + 7 = ☐ 9 + 6 = ☐

4. 4 + 6 = ☐ 3 + 8 = ☐ 8 + 6 = ☐

5. 5 + 8 = ☐ 7 + 9 = ☐ 9 + 4 = ☐

6. 5 + 9 = ☐ 2 + 6 = ☐ 4 + 6 = ☐

☐ 5 9 ☐ 2 6 ☐ 4 6

7. **Write About It** Explain how you can find the total for 5 + 9. What is the total?

____

____

Name

Targeted Practice

Complete the Partner Houses.

1.

10	
+	+
+	+
+	+
+	+
+	

9	
+	+
+	+
+	+
+	+

8	
+	+
+	+
+	+
+	

2.

7	
+	+
+	+
+	+

6	
+	+
+	+
+	

5	
+	+
+	+

3.

4	
+	+
+	

3	
+	+

2	
+	

1-10

Name ____________________

Homework

Stop when I hear 8

Already **5** 6 7 8

5 + [3] = 8

7 8

6

Already **5**

3 more to make 8

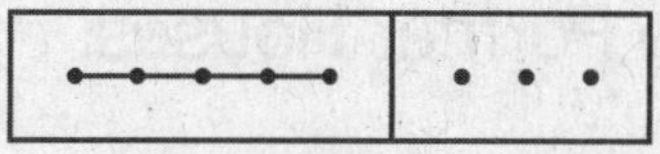

Stop when I hear 8

I took 5 away 6 7 8

3 more to make 8

8 − 5 = [3]

Count on to find the partner.

1. 7 + □ = 9 | 9 − 6 = □ | 3 + □ = 8

2. 5 + □ = 8 | 10 − 7 = □ | 3 + □ = 9

3. 7 + □ = 10 | 10 − 4 = □ | 7 + □ = 11

4. 6 + □ = 8 | 8 − 3 = □ | 6 + □ = 9

5. 2 + □ = 9 | 8 − 6 = □ | 11 − 7 = □

9: 2 and □ | 8: 6 and □ | 11: 7 and □

6. Explain Your Thinking Explain how you found the answer for 11 − 7 = □.

____

____

____

 Name

Remembering

Complete the Partner Houses.

1.

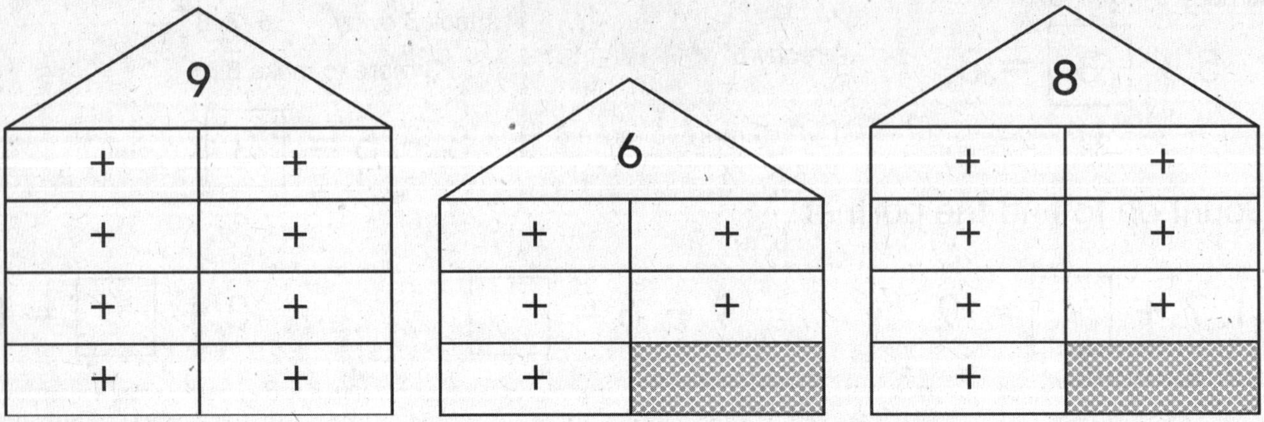

Solve the story problem. **Show your work.**

2. Rachel had 9 toy cars. She gave 7 toy cars to her friends. How many toy cars does Rachel have now?

toy car

☐ ______________
label

Add or subtract 0 or 1.

3. 1 + 8 = ☐ 2 − 0 = ☐ 8 + 1 = ☐

4. 1 + 3 = ☐ 5 − 1 = ☐ 0 + 1 = ☐

5. 1 + 9 = ☐ 6 − 1 = ☐ 9 − 1 = ☐

6. 0 + 5 = ☐ 8 − 0 = ☐ 6 − 0 = ☐

Name ______________________

Homework

Make a ten or count on to find the total.

1. 4 + 8 = ☐ 4 + 6 = ☐ 5 + 7 = ☐

2. 5 + 6 = ☐ 5 + 8 = ☐ 9 + 3 = ☐

3. 3 + 8 = ☐ 7 + 4 = ☐ 9 + 5 = ☐

4. 7 + 7 = ☐ 2 + 8 = ☐ 4 + 9 = ☐

5. 6 + 9 = ☐ 5 + 9 = ☐ 6 + 8 = ☐

6. 6 + 4 = ☐ 8 + 9 = ☐ 6 + 7 = ☐

7. 8 + 2 = ☐ 8 + 3 = ☐ 9 + 9 = ☐

8. 7 + 8 = ☐ 8 + 4 = ☐ 9 + 2 = ☐

9. 8 + 6 = ☐ 7 + 9 = ☐ 5 + 5 = ☐

10. **Explain Your Thinking** Choose one equation above. Explain how you found the total.

____

____

1-11 Name ______________________

Targeted Practice

6 + 3 = 9

Already **6**   • • • 7 8 9

6	• • •
Already **6**	7 8 9

Already **6**

Count on to find the total.

1. 8 + 7 = ☐   2 + 9 = ☐   7 + 5 = ☐

2. 5 + 6 = ☐   3 + 9 = ☐   6 + 9 = ☐

3. 4 + 8 = ☐   4 + 7 = ☐   6 + 6 = ☐

4. 7 + 4 = ☐   3 + 8 = ☐   8 + 4 = ☐

5. 9 + 5 = ☐   4 + 9 = ☐   8 + 5 = ☐

6. 8 + 6 = ☐   7 + 7 = ☐   4 + 8 = ☐

7. 9 + 9 = ☐   6 + 5 = ☐   8 + 8 = ☐

8. **Critical Thinking** How can you use counting on to solve this equation? 7 + 5 = ☐

____

____

Name ______________________

Homework

Make a ten or count on to find the total.

1. 3 + 8 =	4 + 8 =	4 + 9 =
2. 8 + 6 =	9 + 5 =	8 + 5 =
3. 6 + 7 =	7 + 7 =	7 + 5 =
4. 2 + 9 =	5 + 7 =	9 + 2 =
5. 3 + 9 =	8 + 9 =	4 + 7 =
6. 9 + 8 =	7 + 6 =	5 + 9 =
7. 6 + 9 =	6 + 6 =	5 + 6 =
6 9	6 6	5 6

8. **Critical Thinking** Explain how to make a ten to find 8 + 6.

____

____

Remembering

Complete each Partner House.

1.

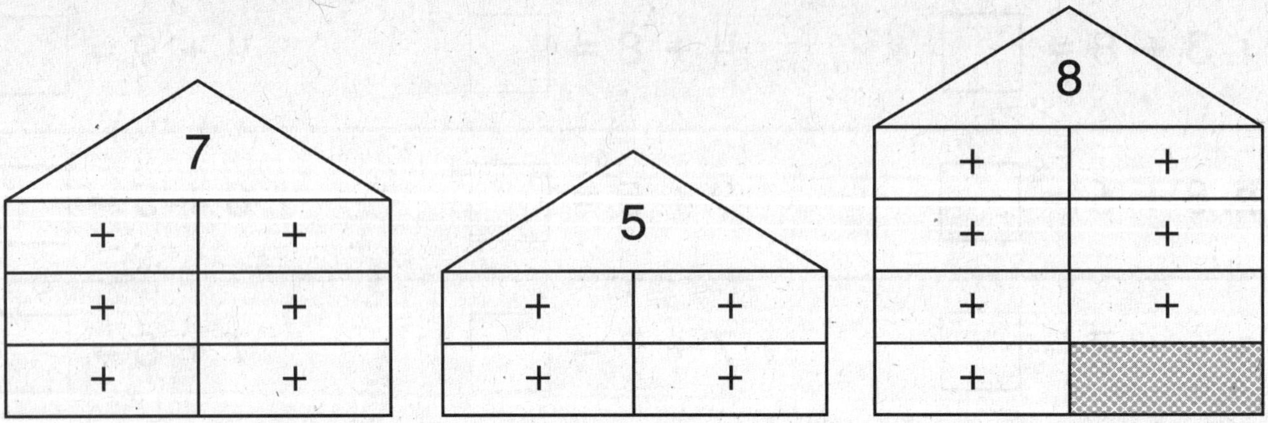

Count on to find the partner.

2. $6 + \square = 10$ $\quad 10 - 7 = \square$ $\quad 3 + \square = 6$

3. $3 + \square = 12$ $\quad 10 - 5 = \square$ $\quad 4 + \square = 7$

4. $4 + \square = 9$ $\quad 13 - 7 = \square$ $\quad 9 + \square = 14$

5. $6 + \square = 8$ $\quad 11 - 4 = \square$ $\quad 8 - 3 = \square$

6. $8 + \square = 13$ $\quad 9 - 6 = \square$ $\quad 11 - 7 = \square$

7. $7 + \square = 9$ $\quad 10 - 8 = \square$ $\quad 11 - 9 = \square$

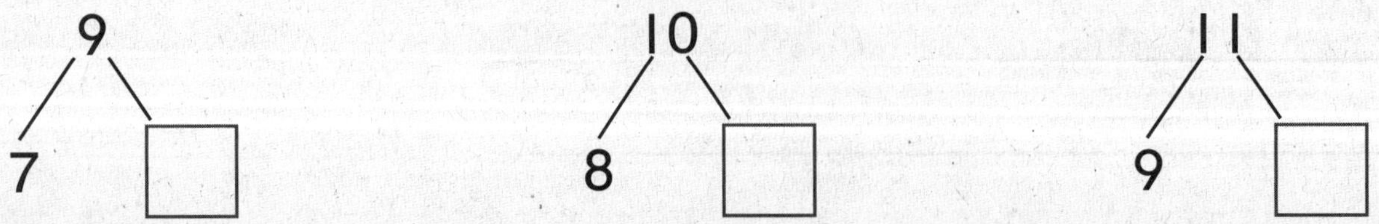

1-13 Name ______________________

Homework

Make a ten or count on to find the total.

1. 3 + 8 = ☐ 4 + 8 = ☐ 4 + 9 = ☐

2. 8 + 6 = ☐ 9 + 5 = ☐ 8 + 5 = ☐

3. 6 + 7 = ☐ 7 + 7 = ☐ 7 + 5 = ☐

4. 7 + 4 = ☐ 8 + 9 = ☐ 4 + 7 = ☐

5. 9 + 8 = ☐ 7 + 6 = ☐ 5 + 9 = ☐

6. 3 + 9 = ☐ 6 + 5 = ☐ 5 + 8 = ☐

7. 6 + 9 = ☐ 6 + 6 = ☐ 5 + 6 = ☐

☐ (6, 9) ☐ (6, 6) ☐ (5, 6)

8. **Critical Thinking** How you can use the Make a Ten strategy to solve 8 + ☐ = 14?

____

____

Name ____________________

Targeted Practice

$8 - 5 = \boxed{3}$

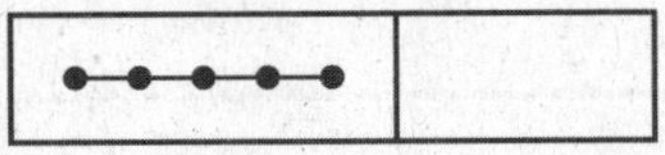

I took away 5   6 7 8

3 more to make 8

or

I took away 5

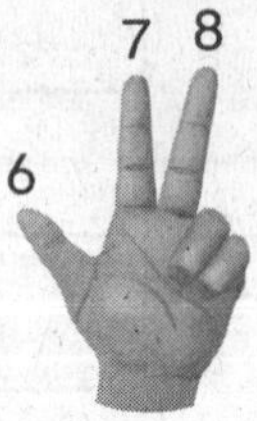

3 more to make 8

Count on to find the partner.

1. $8 - 4 = \square$ $9 - 6 = \square$ $10 - 8 = \square$

2. $7 - 5 = \square$ $10 - 4 = \square$ $6 - 3 = \square$

3. $9 - 3 = \square$ $8 - 5 = \square$ $6 - 5 = \square$

4. $3 - 2 = \square$ $8 - 6 = \square$ $10 - 2 = \square$

3: 2 and $\square$ 8: 6 and $\square$ 10: 2 and $\square$

5. The yard sale records got wet. Some numbers are missing. Fill in the missing numbers.

Item	Number Sold Each Day		
	Saturday	Sunday	Total
Birdhouse	1	6	
Potholder	4		9
Picture Frame	2		10

1–14 **Name** ______

Homework

1. Complete the Math Mountains and equations.

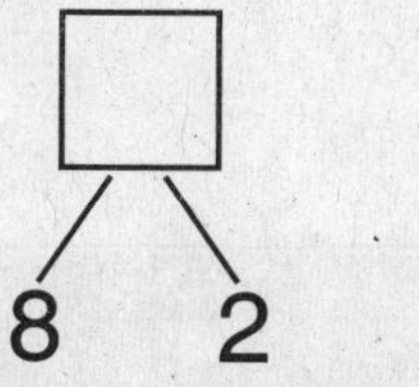

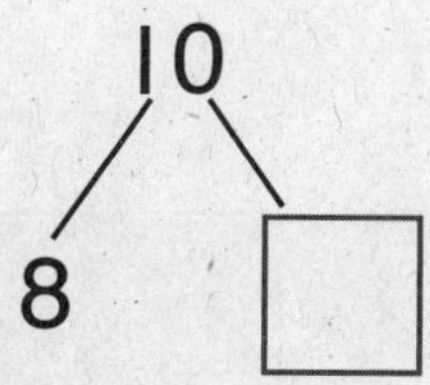

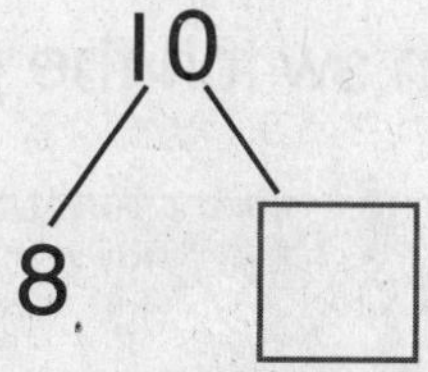

$8 + 2 = \square$ $\qquad$ $8 + \square = 10$ $\qquad$ $10 - 8 = \square$

2. Create and Solve Write and solve a story problem for one of the equations above.

3. Draw a Picture and Explain Draw two different Math Mountains with a total of 12. Explain why you can make two different Math Mountains.

Name ______________________

Remembering

Count the rabbits in the garden.
Write the numbers hidden inside the 10.
Then switch the partners.

1.

10 = ____ + ____

10 = ____ + ____

10 = ____ + ____

10 = ____ + ____

10 = ____ + ____

10 = ____ + ____

Solve the story problems.

Show your work.

2. James had 11 rose bushes. He planted 6 in the back yard and the rest in the front yard. How many rose bushes did he plant in the front yard?

☐ ______________________
label

rose bush

3. Josh had 12 daisies in his hand. He put some in a vase. He has 3 left in his hand. How many daisies did he put in the vase?

☐ ______________________
label

daisies

Name

Homework

8 + [6] = 14 or 14 − 8 = [6]

Already **8** 9 10 11 12 13 14

or **8** 9 10 + 4 more

or **8** + 2 + 4 = 14

or **8** 10 + 4

Already **8**

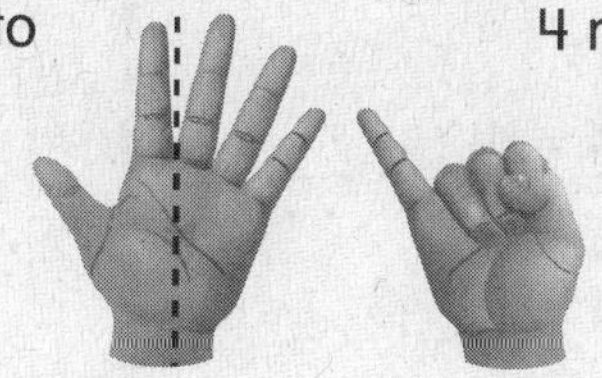

Find the partner.

1. 5 + ☐ = 12	15 − 8 = ☐	8 + ☐ = 16
2. 7 + ☐ = 16	13 − 4 = ☐	9 + ☐ = 12
3. 3 + ☐ = 12	11 − 2 = ☐	7 + ☐ = 13
4. 9 + ☐ = 15	14 − 8 = ☐	17 − 9 = ☐
5. 8 + ☐ = 12	16 − 8 = ☐	16 − 7 = ☐
6. 5 + ☐ = 13	18 − 9 = ☐	12 − 7 = ☐
7. 4 + ☐ = 12	11 − 4 = ☐	12 − 9 = ☐

8. **Explain Your Thinking** Choose one equation above. Explain how you can make a ten to find the partner.

Name ______________________

Targeted Practice

8 + 6 = 14

Already **8** 9 10 11 12 13 14

or **8** 9 10 + 4 more

or **8** + 2 + 4 = 14 (6 splits into 2 and 4)

or **8** 10 + 4 = 14

Already **8**

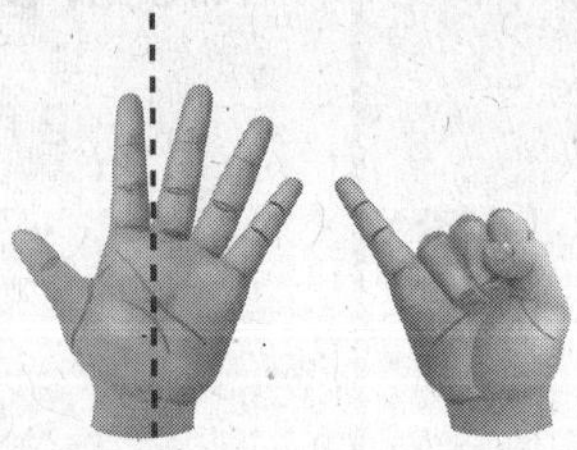

6 gives 2 to 8 to make 10
4 left in 6, so **10 + 4 = 14**

Think 8 + 6
8 + 2 + 4 = 14
10

Make a ten or count on to find the total.

1. 6 + 9 = ☐ 6 + 6 = ☐ 3 + 8 = ☐

2. 6 + 5 = ☐ 5 + 8 = ☐ 6 + 7 = ☐

3. 9 + 8 = ☐ 7 + 6 = ☐ 7 + 4 = ☐

4. 8 + 9 = ☐ 4 + 7 = ☐ 3 + 9 = ☐

5. 2 + 9 = ☐ 5 + 7 = ☐ 8 + 5 = ☐

6. 7 + 7 = ☐ 7 + 5 = ☐ 9 + 2 = ☐

7. 8 + 6 = ☐ 9 + 5 = ☐ 5 + 6 = ☐

8. 4 + 8 = ☐ 4 + 9 = ☐ 5 + 9 = ☐

1–16

Name ____________________

Homework

Write the partner.

1. $6 + \square = 15$	$17 - 8 = \square$	$3 + \square = 11$
2. $9 + \square = 17$	$12 - 6 = \square$	$9 + \square = 12$
3. $5 + \square = 11$	$12 - 4 = \square$	$7 + \square = 12$
4. $8 + \square = 13$	$15 - 7 = \square$	$5 + \square = 14$
5. $7 + \square = 11$	$15 - 8 = \square$	$13 - 7 = \square$
6. $9 + \square = 14$	$13 - 5 = \square$	$11 - 6 = \square$
7. $5 + \square = 12$	$12 - 3 = \square$	$11 - 2 = \square$
8. $8 + \square = 13$	$15 - 9 = \square$	$13 - 6 = \square$
13: 8 and $\square$	15: 9 and $\square$	13: 6 and $\square$

9. **Critical Thinking** Explain how the Proof Drawing can help you solve $8 + \square = 14$.

Already **8** •• | •••• $10 + 4 = 14$

____

____

Name ____________________

Remembering

Solve the story problem. **Show your work.**

1. Ellen has 12 books in her bag.
She put 6 of the books on the table.
How many books are in her bag now?

☐ ____________________
label

book

Complete the Partner Houses.

2.

9	
+	+
+	+
+	+
+	+

7	
+	+
+	+
+	+

5	
+	+
+	+

Write the partner.

3. 5 + ☐ = 11 13 − 9 = ☐ 5 + ☐ = 13

4. 9 + ☐ = 14 12 − 7 = ☐ 8 + ☐ = 14

5. 8 + ☐ = 12 15 − 9 = ☐ 16 − 8 = ☐

6. 7 + ☐ = 13 17 − 8 = ☐ 11 − 4 = ☐

Name

Homework

Count on to find the total or partner.

You can use the number line to help you.

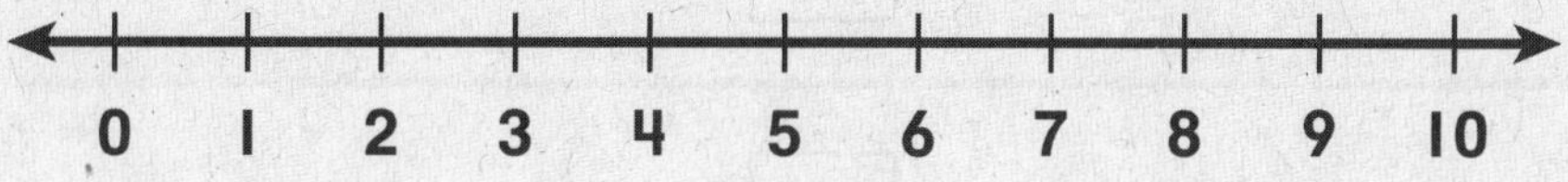

1. $5 + 5 =$ ☐
2. $8 - 3 =$ ☐
3. $7 + 2 =$ ☐
4. $5 - 2 =$ ☐
5. $4 + 1 =$ ☐
6. $7 - 3 =$ ☐
7. $6 - 2 =$ ☐
8. $5 + 4 =$ ☐
9. $9 - 4 =$ ☐
10. $6 + 2 =$ ☐

11. **Write About It** Explain how you would use a number line to solve $3 + 4 =$ ☐.

Name

Targeted Practice

Count on to find the total.

1. 7 + 5 = ☐ 3 + 7 = ☐ 5 + 4 = ☐

2. 9 + 4 = ☐ 2 + 9 = ☐ 8 + 5 = ☐

3. 8 + 6 = ☐ 4 + 6 = ☐ 3 + 6 = ☐

4. 7 + 3 = ☐ 8 + 4 = ☐ 8 + 3 = ☐

5. 6 + 9 = ☐ 4 + 8 = ☐ 5 + 6 = ☐

6. 7 + 8 = ☐ 7 + 7 = ☐ 9 + 3 = ☐

7. 4 + 5 = ☐ 6 + 8 = ☐ 7 + 9 = ☐

Solve the story problem.

Show your work.

8. Gina has 5 crayons. Peter has 6 crayons. How many crayons do they have altogether?

☐ ________
label

crayon

Name ____________________

Homework

$9 + 4 = \boxed{13}$

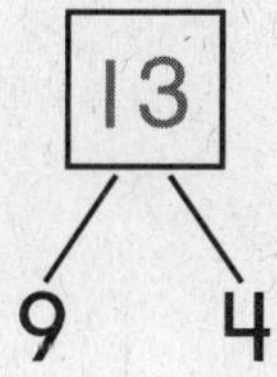

$\begin{array}{r} 9 \\ +\ 4 \\ \hline 13 \end{array}$

I find the total.

$13 - 9 = \boxed{4}$

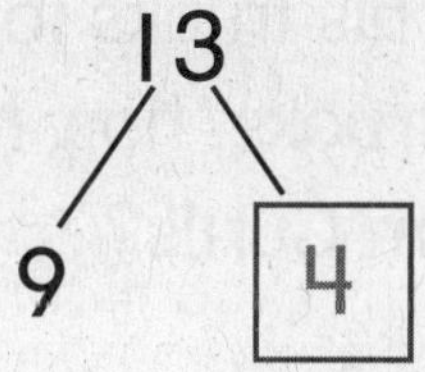

$\begin{array}{r} 13 \\ -\ 9 \\ \hline 4 \end{array}$

I find a partner.

Find the total or partner.

1. $\begin{array}{r} 5 \\ +\ 6 \\ \hline \end{array}$ $\quad \begin{array}{r} 9 \\ +\ 8 \\ \hline \end{array}$ $\quad \begin{array}{r} 8 \\ +\ 3 \\ \hline \end{array}$ $\quad \begin{array}{r} 9 \\ +\ 4 \\ \hline \end{array}$ $\quad \begin{array}{r} 6 \\ +\ 6 \\ \hline \end{array}$ $\quad \begin{array}{r} 8 \\ +\ 6 \\ \hline \end{array}$

2. $\begin{array}{r} 11 \\ -\ 9 \\ \hline \end{array}$ $\quad \begin{array}{r} 14 \\ -\ 6 \\ \hline \end{array}$ $\quad \begin{array}{r} 11 \\ -\ 4 \\ \hline \end{array}$ $\quad \begin{array}{r} 13 \\ -\ 5 \\ \hline \end{array}$ $\quad \begin{array}{r} 12 \\ -\ 3 \\ \hline \end{array}$ $\quad \begin{array}{r} 16 \\ -\ 9 \\ \hline \end{array}$

3. $\begin{array}{r} 16 \\ -\ 8 \\ \hline \end{array}$ $\quad \begin{array}{r} 15 \\ -\ 7 \\ \hline \end{array}$ $\quad \begin{array}{r} 12 \\ -\ 5 \\ \hline \end{array}$ $\quad \begin{array}{r} 11 \\ -\ 2 \\ \hline \end{array}$ $\quad \begin{array}{r} 17 \\ -\ 9 \\ \hline \end{array}$ $\quad \begin{array}{r} 16 \\ -\ 7 \\ \hline \end{array}$

4. Draw a Math Mountain to solve for $16 - 7 = \square$.

Name ____________________

Remembering

Solve the story problem.	Show your work.
1. Yesterday John bought 8 trucks. Today Curtis gave some of his trucks to John. If John now has 15 trucks, how many trucks did he get from Curtis? ☐ ____________ label	

Complete the Partner Houses.

2.

7	
+	+
+	+
+	+

6	
+	+
+	+
+	

9	
+	+
+	+
+	+
+	+

Make a ten or count on to find the total or partner.

3. 9 + ☐ = 13   11 − 2 = ☐   7 + 4 = ☐

4. 2 + ☐ = 11   11 − 6 = ☐   9 + 8 = ☐

5. 5 + ☐ = 14   13 − 6 = ☐   7 + 8 = ☐

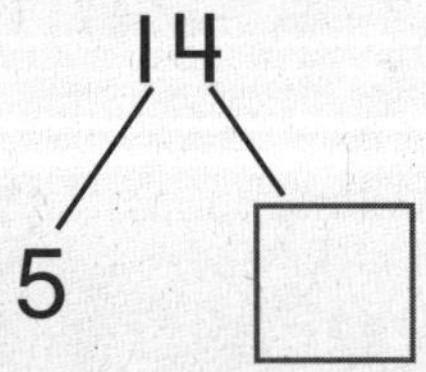

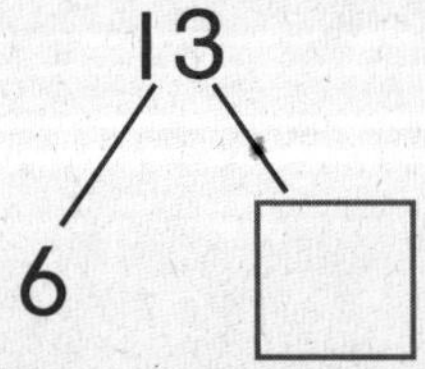

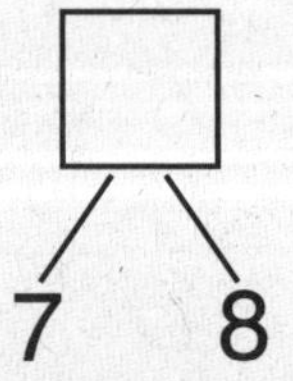

Name ______________________

Homework

Find the total or the partner. Draw squiggles under the partners.

1. $5 + 9 = \square$ $\quad 5 + \square = 14$ $\quad 14 - 5 = \square$

2. $9 + 6 = \square$ $\quad 9 + \square = 15$ $\quad 15 - 9 = \square$

3. $4 + 7 = \square$ $\quad 4 + \square = 11$ $\quad 11 - 4 = \square$

4. $6 + 5 = \square$ $\quad 6 + \square = 11$ $\quad 11 - 6 = \square$

5. $5 + 7 = \square$ $\quad 5 + \square = 12$ $\quad 12 - 5 = \square$

6. $8 + 6 = \square$ $\quad 8 + \square = 14$ $\quad 14 - 8 = \square$

7. $3 + 9 = \square$ $\quad 3 + \square = 12$ $\quad 12 - 3 = \square$

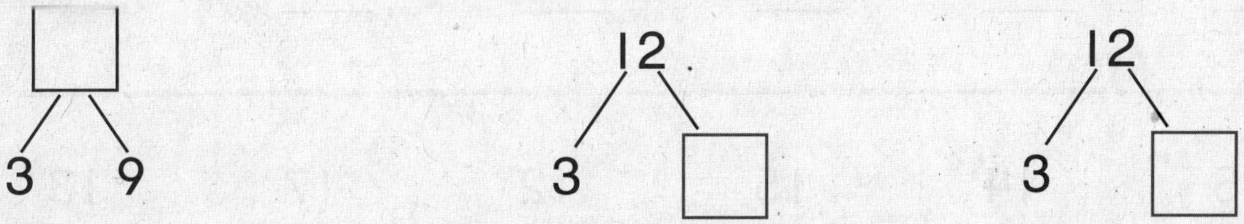

8. **Write Your Own** Write an equation to show that an unknown number is added to 4 and the total is 13. Write and solve a story problem that uses your equation.

____

____

____

Name ____________________

Targeted Practice

$9 + 4 = \boxed{13}$

13 (boxed) → 9, 4

$\begin{array}{r} 9 \\ +4 \\ \hline 13 \end{array}$

$13 - 9 = \boxed{4}$

13 → 9, 4 (boxed)

$\begin{array}{r} 13 \\ -9 \\ \hline 4 \end{array}$

Add or subtract.

1. $\begin{array}{r} 5 \\ +6 \\ \hline \end{array}$ $\begin{array}{r} 9 \\ +3 \\ \hline \end{array}$ $\begin{array}{r} 8 \\ +3 \\ \hline \end{array}$ $\begin{array}{r} 2 \\ +9 \\ \hline \end{array}$ $\begin{array}{r} 6 \\ +6 \\ \hline \end{array}$ $\begin{array}{r} 8 \\ +6 \\ \hline \end{array}$

2. $\begin{array}{r} 9 \\ +6 \\ \hline \end{array}$ $\begin{array}{r} 4 \\ +8 \\ \hline \end{array}$ $\begin{array}{r} 3 \\ +9 \\ \hline \end{array}$ $\begin{array}{r} 7 \\ +5 \\ \hline \end{array}$ $\begin{array}{r} 8 \\ +7 \\ \hline \end{array}$ $\begin{array}{r} 7 \\ +7 \\ \hline \end{array}$

3. $\begin{array}{r} 17 \\ -9 \\ \hline \end{array}$ $\begin{array}{r} 14 \\ -6 \\ \hline \end{array}$ $\begin{array}{r} 16 \\ -7 \\ \hline \end{array}$ $\begin{array}{r} 15 \\ -8 \\ \hline \end{array}$ $\begin{array}{r} 11 \\ -6 \\ \hline \end{array}$ $\begin{array}{r} 14 \\ -8 \\ \hline \end{array}$

4. $\begin{array}{r} 15 \\ -9 \\ \hline \end{array}$ $\begin{array}{r} 14 \\ -7 \\ \hline \end{array}$ $\begin{array}{r} 15 \\ -7 \\ \hline \end{array}$ $\begin{array}{r} 12 \\ -7 \\ \hline \end{array}$ $\begin{array}{r} 17 \\ -8 \\ \hline \end{array}$ $\begin{array}{r} 13 \\ -7 \\ \hline \end{array}$

5. $\begin{array}{r} 18 \\ -9 \\ \hline \end{array}$ $\begin{array}{r} 7 \\ +6 \\ \hline \end{array}$ $\begin{array}{r} 16 \\ -9 \\ \hline \end{array}$ $\begin{array}{r} 8 \\ +9 \\ \hline \end{array}$ $\begin{array}{r} 5 \\ +8 \\ \hline \end{array}$ $\begin{array}{r} 14 \\ -5 \\ \hline \end{array}$

Name ______________________________

Homework

$9 + 4 = \boxed{13}$

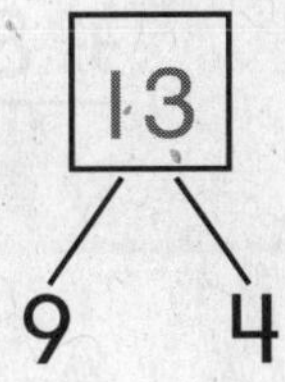

$$\begin{array}{r} 9 \\ +\ 4 \\ \hline 13 \end{array}$$

$13 - 9 = \boxed{4}$

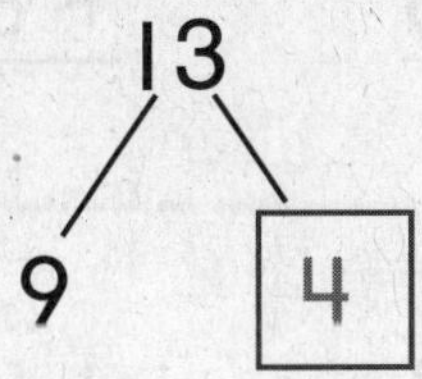

$$\begin{array}{r} 13 \\ -\ 9 \\ \hline 4 \end{array}$$

Write the partner or total.

1. $\begin{array}{r} 9 \\ +\ 3 \\ \hline \end{array}$ $\begin{array}{r} 5 \\ +\ 6 \\ \hline \end{array}$ $\begin{array}{r} 7 \\ +\ 8 \\ \hline \end{array}$ $\begin{array}{r} 5 \\ +\ 8 \\ \hline \end{array}$ $\begin{array}{r} 4 \\ +\ 8 \\ \hline \end{array}$ $\begin{array}{r} 7 \\ +\ 4 \\ \hline \end{array}$

2. $\begin{array}{r} 5 \\ +\ 9 \\ \hline \end{array}$ $\begin{array}{r} 9 \\ +\ 6 \\ \hline \end{array}$ $\begin{array}{r} 8 \\ +\ 6 \\ \hline \end{array}$ $\begin{array}{r} 6 \\ +\ 9 \\ \hline \end{array}$ $\begin{array}{r} 9 \\ +\ 7 \\ \hline \end{array}$ $\begin{array}{r} 8 \\ +\ 9 \\ \hline \end{array}$

3. $\begin{array}{r} 15 \\ -\ 9 \\ \hline \end{array}$ $\begin{array}{r} 11 \\ -\ 8 \\ \hline \end{array}$ $\begin{array}{r} 13 \\ -\ 4 \\ \hline \end{array}$ $\begin{array}{r} 14 \\ -\ 5 \\ \hline \end{array}$ $\begin{array}{r} 11 \\ -\ 3 \\ \hline \end{array}$ $\begin{array}{r} 11 \\ -\ 6 \\ \hline \end{array}$

4. Create Your Own Write and solve a story problem for this equation, $8 + \square = 12$.

____

____

____

Name ________________________

Remembering

Add or subtract.

1.	8 + 3	7 + 5	4 + 8	9 + 9	9 + 3	6 + 8
2.	4 + 7	7 + 6	8 + 8	13 − 4	14 − 9	15 − 7
3.	15 − 8	14 − 7	11 − 5	11 − 2	16 − 9	18 − 9

Write all of the equations for the 13, 5, 8 Math Mountain. Draw squiggles under the partners.

13

5 8

4. 5 + 8 = 13 ____________ 13 = 5 + 8 ____________

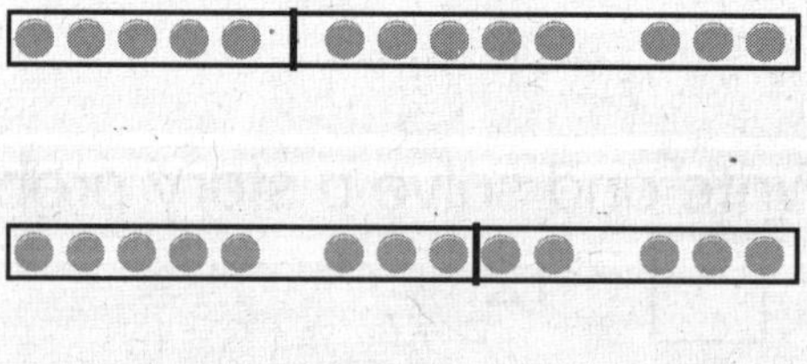

____________ ____________

____________ ____________

____________ ____________

Name ______________________________

Homework

Compare. Write < or >.

1. 4 ◯ 8
2. 10 ◯ 6
3. 9 ◯ 12
4. 15 ◯ 17
5. 14 ◯ 13
6. 19 ◯ 18
7. 16 ◯ 10
8. 5 ◯ 11
9. 7 ◯ 9

Write each set of numbers in order from least to greatest.

10. 8 5 10

    ____ ____ ____

11. 18 12 6

    ____ ____ ____

12. 19 14 15

    ____ ____ ____

Write each set of numbers in order from greatest to least.

13. 4 12 9

    ____ ____ ____

14. 11 3 13

    ____ ____ ____

15. 9 19 16

    ____ ____ ____

16. **Logical Thinking** Use the clues and numbers in the box to solve the problem.

    Kyle has more hats than Sue.
    Kim has the most hats.
    How many hats does each child have?

9 5 8

    Kyle ____________ Kim ____________ Sue ____________

Name ______________________

Targeted Practice

Find all of the equations for the Math Mountains.
Draw squiggles under the partners.

15
7 8

1. 7 + 8 = 15 ______ 15 = 7 + 8 ______

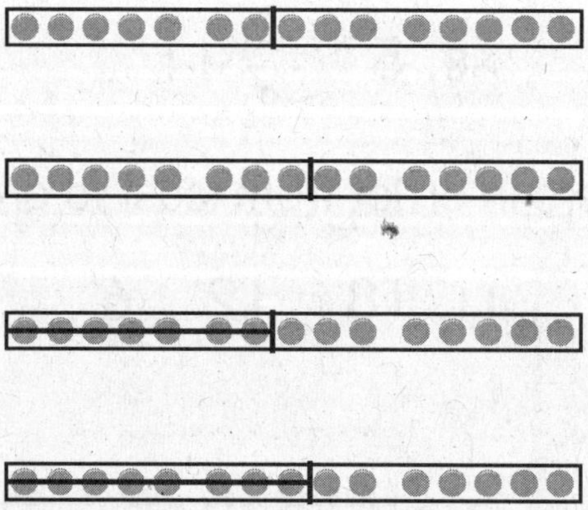

______ ______

______ ______

______ ______

11
4 7

2. 4 + 7 = 11 ______ 11 = 4 + 7 ______

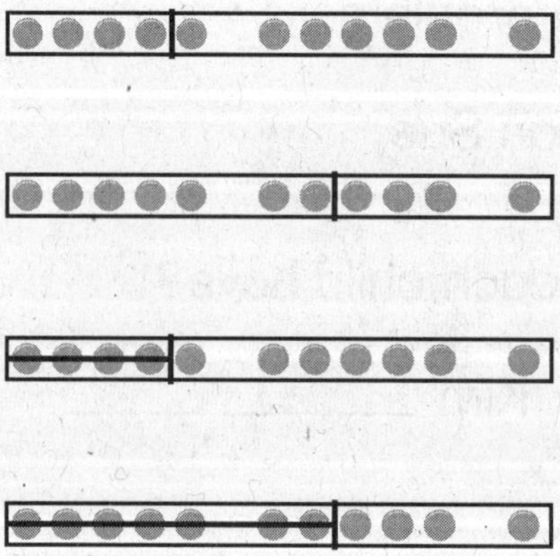

______ ______

______ ______

______ ______

Name ______________________

Homework

$$5 + 2 + 3 = \square$$

You can add in three different ways.

7 + 3	5 + 5	8 + 2
5 + 2 + 3 = 10	5 + 2 + 3 = 10	5 + 2 + 3 = 10

Add the three numbers.

1. 4 + 7 + 3 = ☐ 5 + 1 + 3 = ☐ 6 + 3 + 4 = ☐
2. 6 + 2 + 8 = ☐ 4 + 2 + 6 = ☐ 7 + 7 + 3 = ☐
3. 3 + 4 + 7 = ☐ 5 + 9 + 2 = ☐ 4 + 3 + 9 = ☐
4. 7 + 3 + 5 = ☐ 2 + 4 + 4 = ☐ 7 + 1 + 7 = ☐
5. 3 + 6 + 3 = ☐ 2 + 2 + 9 = ☐ 6 + 1 + 3 = ☐
6. 5 + 5 + 5 = ☐ 2 + 7 + 2 = ☐ 9 + 2 + 5 = ☐
7. **Explain Your Thinking** Draw a 7, 9, 16 Math Mountain. Tell how it can help you add or subtract.

____

____

____

Name ____________________

Remembering

Solve the story problem. | **Show your work.**

1. Nancy rode her bike 7 miles. Yolanda rode her bike 6 more miles than Nancy. How many miles did Yolanda ride her bike?

☐ ____________________
label

Add or subtract 0 or 1.

2. 2 + 0 = ☐ 5 − 1 = ☐ 5 + 0 = ☐ 4 − 1 = ☐

3. 7 + 1 = ☐ 6 − 0 = ☐ 3 + 0 = ☐ 1 − 1 = ☐

4. 8 + 1 = ☐ 8 − 0 = ☐ 9 + 1 = ☐ 3 − 1 = ☐

Find all of the equations for the 11, 7, 4 Math Mountain.
Draw squiggles under the partners.

5.

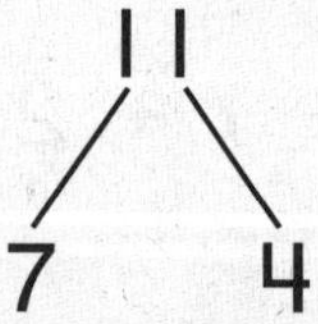

7 + 4 = 11

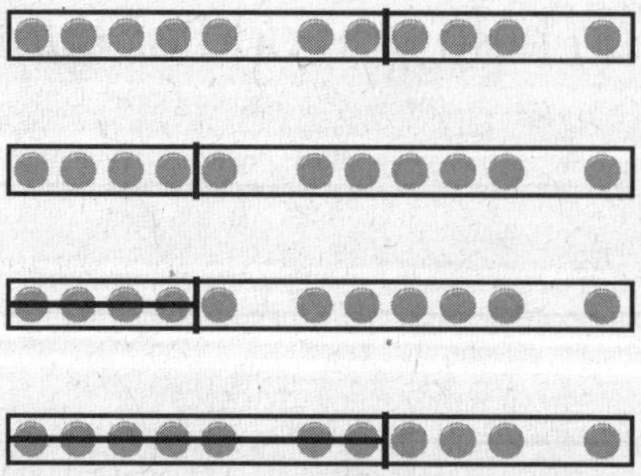

11 = 7 + 4

____

____

____

____

____

____

Name ____________________

Homework

1. Measure the horizontal line segment below by marking and counting 1-cm lengths.

______________________ ☐ cm

2. Draw a line segment 8 cm long. Mark and count 1-cm lengths to check the length.

Use your centimeter ruler to measure each vertical line segment.

3. ☐ cm

4. ☐ cm

5. ☐ cm

---

6. **On the Back** Draw a 7-cm line segment. Draw all the partner lengths. Write the partners and the equation for each.

Name ______________________________

A–2

Name ______________________

Homework

Look for rectangles, squares, and triangles in your home and neighborhood.

1. List or draw objects that show squares.

2. List or draw objects that show rectangles.

3. List or draw objects that show triangles.

4. On the Back Draw a square, a rectangle, and a triangle.

Name ______________________________

Name

A-3

Name

Homework

Use a centimeter ruler. Find the perimeter.

1.

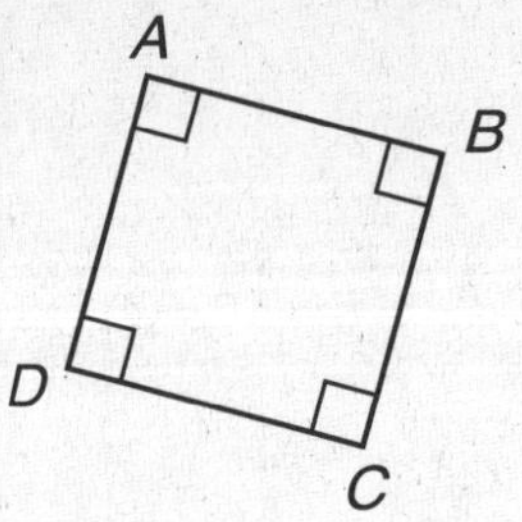

$P =$ ☐ cm

2.

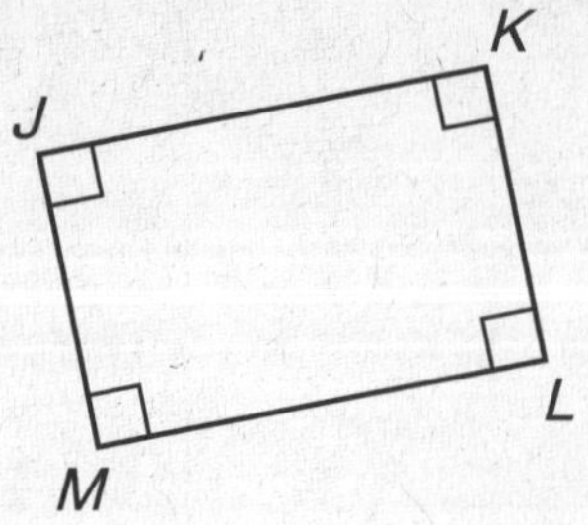

$P =$ ☐ cm

3.

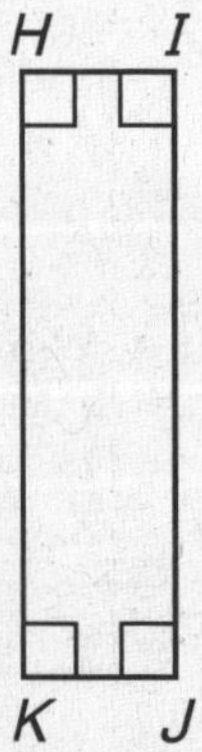

$P =$ ☐ cm

4.

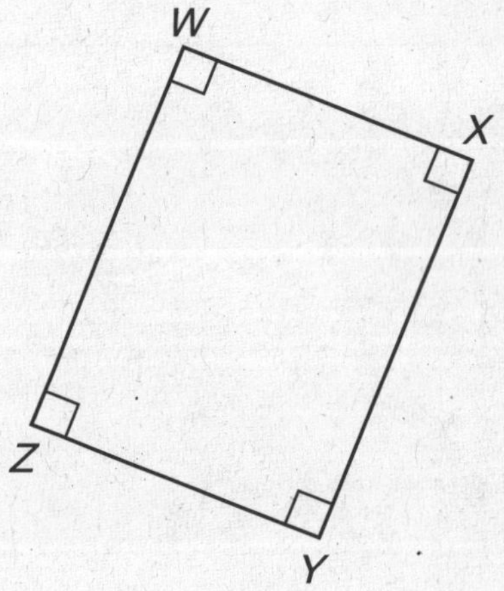

$P =$ ☐ cm

5. On the Back Draw a square and a rectangle. Find the perimeter of each shape.

Name ____________________

Homework

Use a centimeter ruler. Find the perimeter.

1.

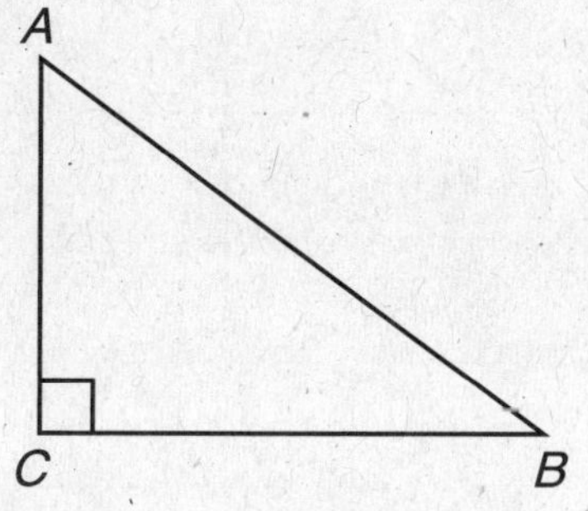

$P =$ ☐ cm

2.

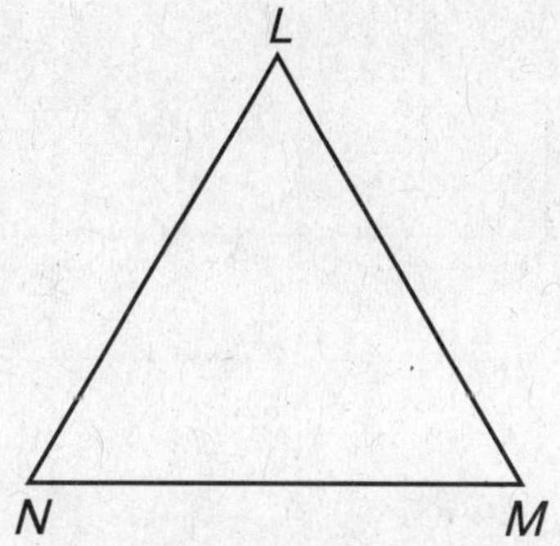

$P =$ ☐ cm

Measure. Round to the nearest centimeter.

3. ____________________ about ☐ cm

4. ____ about ☐ cm

Measure each side. Round to the nearest centimeter.
Find the perimeter.

5.

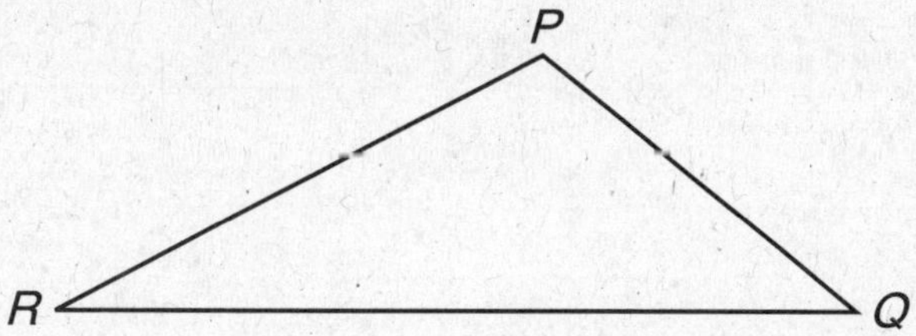

Perimeter is about ☐ cm

6.

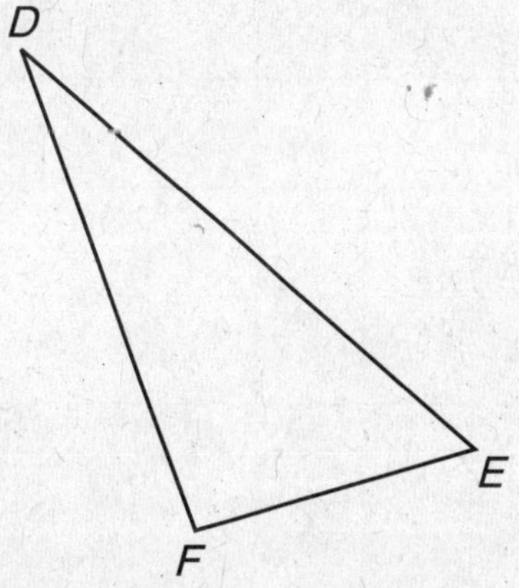

Perimeter is about ☐ cm

7. On the Back Use a centimeter ruler. Draw three triangles. Find the perimeter of each triangle.

Name ____________________

2–1

Name ______________________

Homework

Solve the story problems.

Show your work.

1. Brad had 14 toy boats. 5 of them floated away. How many does he have now?

☐ ______________________
label

boat

2. Moses collected 17 rocks. He gave some of them away. Now he has 9 rocks left. How many did he give away?

☐ ______________________
label

rock

3. Claire had 9 colored markers in her backpack when she left school. Some fell out on the way home. When she got home, she had only 5 markers. How many markers fell out of her backpack?

☐ ______________________
label

backpack

4. A honeybee visited 7 flowers in the garden. Then it visited 5 more. How many flowers did the honeybee visit in all?

☐ ______________________
label

honeybee

 Name ______________________

Remembering

1. Find all of the equations for the 15, 7, 8 Math Mountain. Draw squiggles under each partner.

15
7 8

7 + 8 = 15 ______________ 15 = 7 + 8

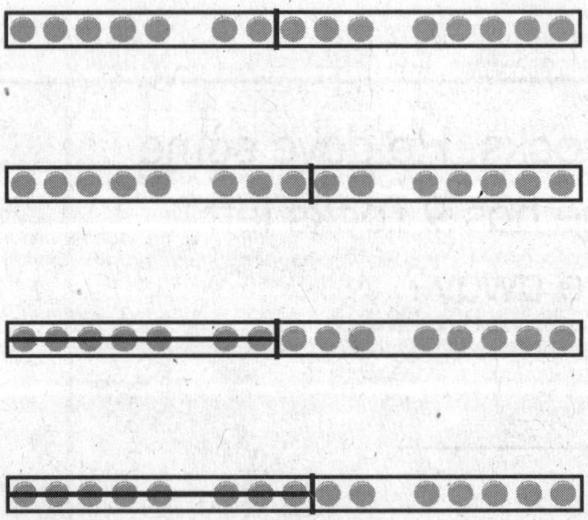

______________ ______________

______________ ______________

______________ ______________

Add 3 numbers.

2. 4 + 1 + 4 = ☐ 5 + 1 + 1 = ☐ 2 + 2 + 4 = ☐

3. 5 + 2 + 2 = ☐ 4 + 1 + 3 = ☐ 2 + 3 + 2 = ☐

Add or subtract.

4. $\begin{array}{r} 6 \\ +\ 7 \\ \hline \end{array}$ $\begin{array}{r} 8 \\ +\ 8 \\ \hline \end{array}$ $\begin{array}{r} 5 \\ +\ 9 \\ \hline \end{array}$ $\begin{array}{r} 11 \\ -\ 3 \\ \hline \end{array}$ $\begin{array}{r} 17 \\ -\ 8 \\ \hline \end{array}$ $\begin{array}{r} 14 \\ -\ 6 \\ \hline \end{array}$

5. Measurement Use your centimeter ruler. On a separate piece of paper, draw a square. Find its perimeter.

2–2

Homework

Name ____________________

Draw a Proof Drawing to solve the story problems.

Show your work.

1. In the morning, Nick made 8 animals out of clay. In the afternoon, he made some more clay animals. Altogether, he made 15 clay animals. How many did he make in the afternoon?

clay animal

☐ ____________________
label

2. Carrie saw some birds in a tree. 8 flew away. 5 were left. How many birds were in the tree first?

bird

☐ ____________________
label

3. Leon and his friends made 12 snowmen. The next day, Leon saw that some of them had melted. Only 9 snowmen were left. How many melted?

snowmen

☐ ____________________
label

4. 3 lizards sat on a rock in the sun. Then 9 more came out and sat on the rock. How many lizards are on the rock now?

rock

☐ ____________________
label

2–2 Name

Targeted Practice

$5 + 4 + 3 = \square$

9 + 3 5 + 4 + 3 = 12	5 + 7 5 + 4 + 3 = 12	8 + 4 5 + 4 + 3 = 12

Add.

1. $4 + 8 + 3 = \square$ $8 + 8 + 2 = \square$ $7 + 7 + 3 = \square$

2. $8 + 2 + 6 = \square$ $5 + 4 + 9 = \square$ $9 + 2 + 5 = \square$

3. $7 + 5 + 2 = \square$ $8 + 4 + 2 = \square$ $6 + 9 + 4 = \square$

4. $9 + 3 + 4 = \square$ $9 + 4 + 5 = \square$ $8 + 4 + 4 = \square$

5. $5 + 8 + 2 = \square$ $2 + 9 + 6 = \square$ $6 + 3 + 7 = \square$

6. $2 + 7 + 2 = \square$ $5 + 4 + 5 = \square$ $8 + 2 + 7 = \square$

7. $3 + 6 + 3 = \square$ $9 + 2 + 2 = \square$ $5 + 7 + 3 = \square$

8. $2 + 6 + 4 = \square$ $6 + 3 + 4 = \square$ $4 + 5 + 3 = \square$

9. $2 + 7 + 3 = \square$ $4 + 2 + 5 = \square$ $5 + 3 + 3 = \square$

2–3 Name

Homework

Draw a Proof Drawing to solve the story problems.

Show your work.

1. There are some pigs on Mr. Smith's farm. 8 of them are eating corn. The other 7 are drinking water. How many pigs are on Mr. Smith's farm?

   ☐ ____________

   label

pig

2. Wendy bought 3 blue balloons and some red balloons for a party. She bought 11 balloons. How many red ones did she buy?

   ☐ ____________

   label

balloon

3. There are 14 children in the park. 7 of them are swinging. The rest are jumping rope. How many are jumping rope?

   ☐ ____________

   label

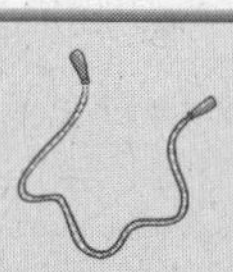

jump rope

4. **Write Your Own** Write a collection story problem. Then draw a picture to solve it.

   ____

   ____

   ____

Name ______________________

Remembering

Complete the Partner Houses.

1.

7	
+	+
+	+
+	+

9	
+	+
+	+
+	+
+	+

6	
+	+
+	+
+	

Add or subtract.

2.	4 + 7	5 + 6	7 + 8	8 + 6	7 + 7	9 + 5
3.	6 + 9	7 + 6	8 + 8	9 + 7	6 + 8	5 + 8
4.	13 − 8	12 − 7	17 − 9	14 − 6	15 − 7	16 − 8
5.	11 − 3	15 − 8	18 − 9	13 − 4	16 − 9	14 − 7

6. Measurement Use your centimeter ruler. On a separate piece of paper, draw a segment 6 centimeters long. Draw all of its partner lengths.

Name ____________________

Homework

Solve the story problems. **Show your work.**

1. One bus has 6 girls and 7 boys on it. How many students are on the bus?

☐ ____________________
label

bus

2. Pang bought some apples. Bill bought 6 pears. Pang and Bill bought 13 pieces of fruit. How many apples did Pang buy?

☐ ____________________
label

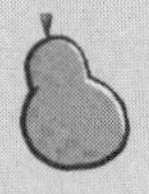

pear

3. Complete the Venn diagram by adding at least two things in the circle.

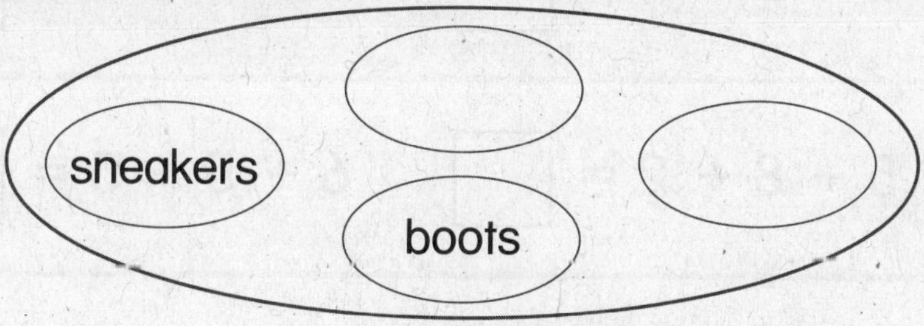

____
Group Name

4. Create Your Own Use your Venn diagram to write your own group name story problem. Solve your problem with equations,words, or Proof Drawings.

____

____

____

Name ______________________

Targeted Practice

2 + 3 + 6 = ☐

5 + 6 2 + 3 + 6 = 11	2 + 9 2 + 3 + 6 = 11	8 + 3 2 + 3 + 6 = 11

Add.

1. 5 + 7 + 3 = ☐ 7 + 3 + 2 = ☐ 9 + 2 + 6 = ☐

2. 8 + 2 + 5 = ☐ 6 + 2 + 5 = ☐ 3 + 5 + 6 = ☐

3. 4 + 3 + 4 = ☐ 5 + 3 + 4 = ☐ 8 + 3 + 2 = ☐

4. 6 + 3 + 9 = ☐ 7 + 7 + 2 = ☐ 2 + 5 + 8 = ☐

5. 2 + 7 + 3 = ☐ 5 + 8 + 2 = ☐ 6 + 5 + 5 = ☐

6. 8 + 2 + 2 = ☐ 7 + 4 + 6 = ☐ 4 + 3 + 7 = ☐

7. 5 + 6 + 4 = ☐ 3 + 4 + 4 = ☐ 5 + 2 + 9 = ☐

8. 2 + 8 + 4 = ☐ 6 + 4 + 4 = ☐ 7 + 2 + 4 = ☐

9. 6 + 2 + 3 = ☐ 4 + 5 + 5 = ☐ 9 + 3 + 4 = ☐

Name ______________________________

Homework

Draw a picture to solve the story problems. **Show your work.**

1. Peter has 13 eggs. Joe has 4 fewer than Peter. How many eggs does Joe have?

☐ ____________________
label

eggs

2. I want to give each of my 14 friends a watermelon. I have 8 watermelons in my garden. How many more do I need to grow to give each friend a watermelon?

☐ ____________________
label

watermelon

3. Lë has 5 lemons. Tina has 7 more than Lë. How many lemons does Tina have?

☐ ____________________
label

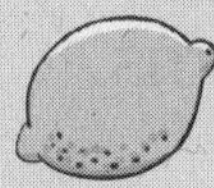

lemon

Write Your Own Complete this comparison story problem. Then draw a picture to show how to solve it.

4. I have 12 ____________________.
My friend has ____________________ fewer ____________________ than I have. How many ____________________ does my friend have?

☐ ____________________
label

2–5 **Name** ______________________

Remembering

Find all of the equations for the 13, 4, and 9 Math Mountain. Draw squiggles under the partners.

1.

13

4 9

$4 + 9 = 13$

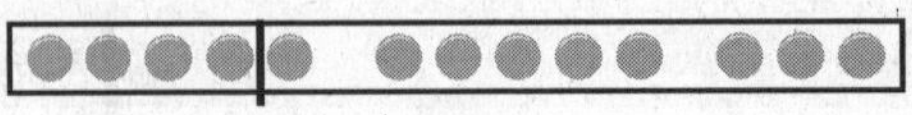

$13 = 4 + 9$

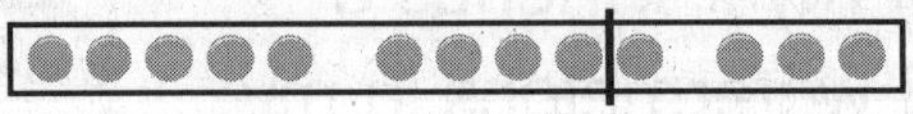

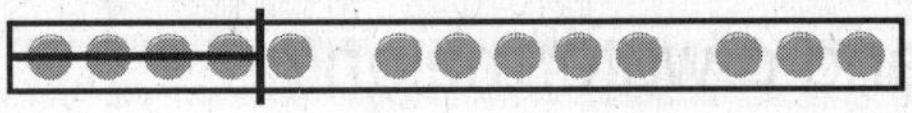

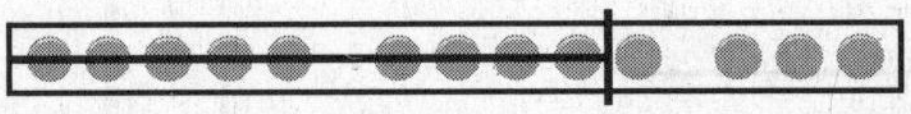

Solve the story problems. **Show your work.**

2. 8 peppers are growing in Dana's garden. Dana has 9 peppers in the kitchen. How many peppers does Dana have altogether?

☐ ______________ label

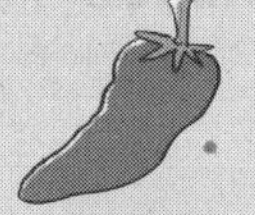

3. Jonathan had 14 files on his CD. Then he deleted 6. How many files were left?

☐ ______________ label

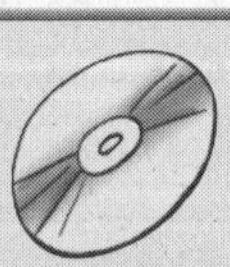

4. Measurement Use your centimeter ruler. On a separate piece of paper, draw a rectangle. Find its perimeter.

2-6

Homework

Name ______________________

Solve the story problems.

Show your work.

1. Parker and Natu went to the store to buy sunglasses. Parker paid $9 for his sunglasses. Natu paid $6 more than Parker. How much did Natu pay for his sunglasses?

sunglasses

☐ ______________

label

2. A small ball costs 8 cents. A ring costs 8 more cents than the small ball. How many cents does a ring cost?

ring

☐ ______________

label

3. If Jared gives away 3 strawberries, Jared will have as many strawberries as Phil. Phil has 8 strawberries. How many strawberries does Jared have?

strawberries

☐ ______________

label

4. Andrew has 11 soccer balls. William has 3 soccer balls. How many fewer soccer balls does William have than Andrew?

soccer ball

☐ ______________

label

2–6 **Name** ____________________

Targeted Practice

Fill in the Venn diagrams to show some things that belong together.

1.

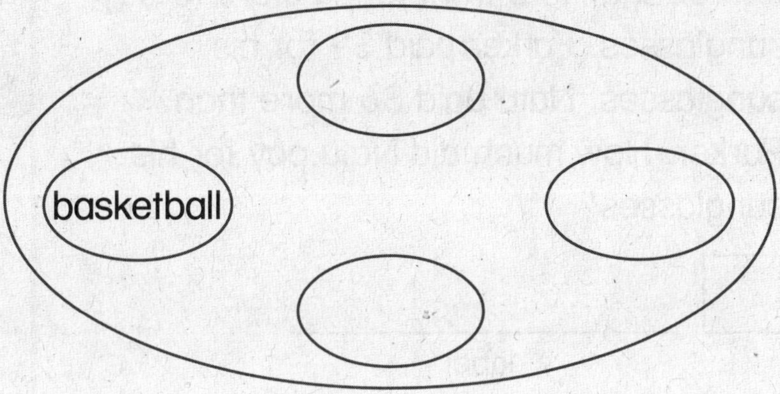

____

Group Name

2.

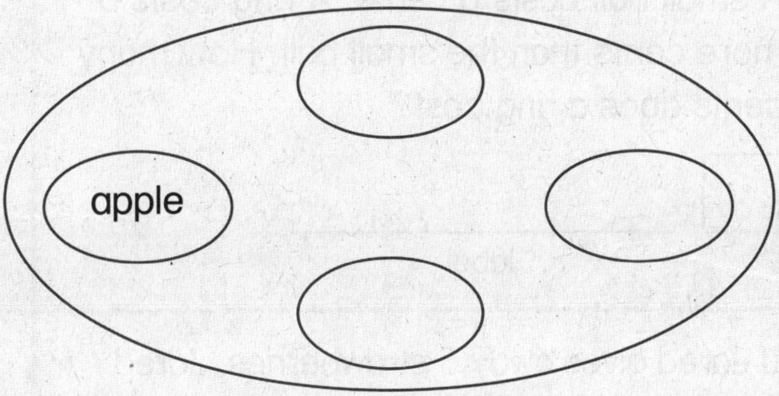

____

Group Name

3. You Decide Create your own Venn diagram. Write a group name.

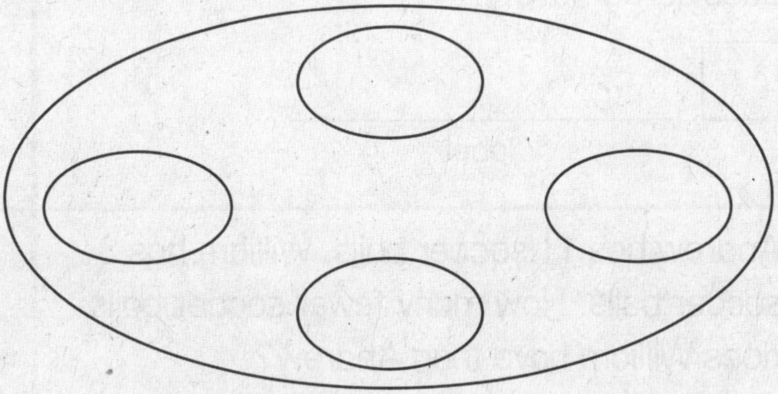

____

Group Name

Name ______________________

Homework

Solve the story problems. **Show your work.**

1. Susan rode her bicycle for 14 blocks. Awan rode his bicycle for 8 blocks. How many fewer blocks did Awan ride than Susan?

bicycle

☐ ______________ label

2. Eden has 7 blackberries. Her father gave her 9 more. How many blackberries does Eden have now?

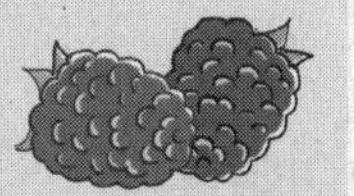

blackberries

☐ ______________ label

3. There were 9 children on the bus. At the first bus stop, some children got off. 7 children are still on the bus. How many children got off at the first bus stop?

bus stop

☐ ______________ label

4. The clown had 12 balloons. He gave away 4 balloons. How many balloons did he keep?

balloons

☐ ______________ label

Name ______________________

Remembering

Add or subtract.

1. 4 + 1 = ☐ 3 − 0 = ☐ 6 + 0 = ☐ 9 − 1 = ☐

2. 8 + 0 = ☐ 7 − 1 = ☐ 9 + 1 = ☐ 4 − 0 = ☐

3. 7 + 1 = ☐ 5 − 0 = ☐ 4 + 0 = ☐ 8 − 1 = ☐

Solve the story problem. **Show your work.**

4. Mr. Tyson grilled 14 hot dogs. His family ate some. Now he has 6 hot dogs left. How many hot dogs did his family eat?

☐ ______________________
label

hot dog

Complete the Partner Houses.

5.

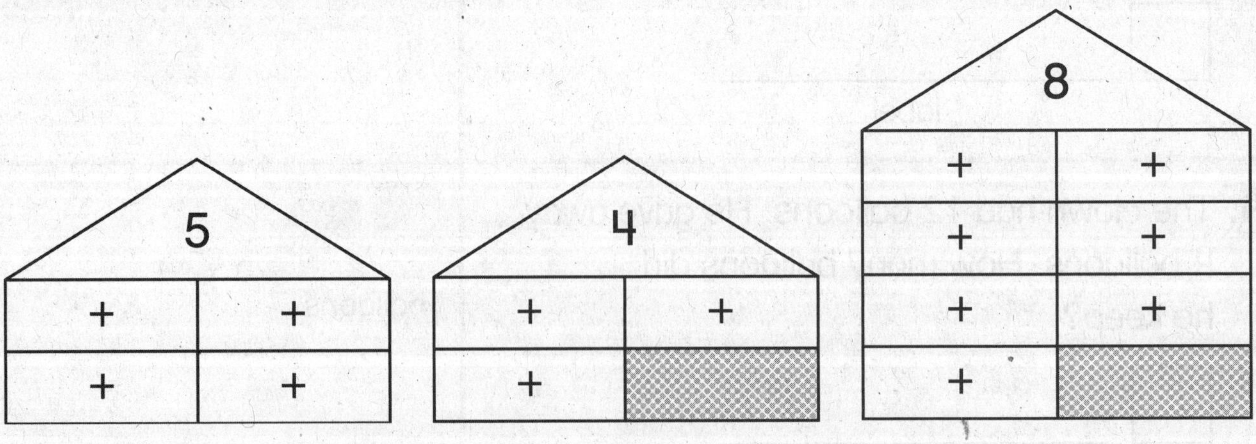

6. **Measurement** Use your centimeter ruler. On a separate piece of paper, draw a triangle. Find its perimeter.

2–8

Name ______

Homework

For problems with not enough information, add the information.

For problems with extra information, cross out the extra information. Then solve the problem.

Show your work.

1. There are 14 children in music class. Some children left to go to the library. How many children are still in music class?

library

______

☐ ______
label

2. Rosa has 5 gold coins and 6 silver coins in her collection. Her brother gave her 7 more gold coins. How many gold coins does Rosa have in all?

coin

______

☐ ______
label

3. There were 7 bicycles in the rack at school. Then some more children put their bicycles in the rack. How many bicycles are in the rack now?

bicycle

______

☐ ______
label

Name ______________________

Targeted Practice

Solve the story problems. | **Show your work.**

1. Bernard had 9 acorns. Manuel had 6 fewer acorns than Bernard. How many acorns does Manuel have?

☐ ______________ label

2. Together Roma and Grace have 12 beads. Grace has 4 beads. How many beads does Grace have to buy to have the same as Roma?

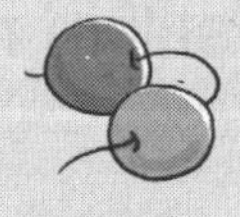

☐ ______________ label

3. There are 14 lions at the zoo. The zoo has to get 6 tigers to have as many tigers as lions. How many tigers does the zoo have?

☐ ______________ label

4. There are 13 children on the baseball team. There are 7 children on the swim team. How many more children are on the baseball team than on the swim team?

☐ ______________ label

Name ______________________________

Homework

Cross out the extra information. Write hidden or missing information. Then solve the problems.

Show your work.

1. Joel knows the names of 9 different dinosaurs. His friend Peja knows the names of 6 dinosaurs and 8 birds. How many dinosaur names do the two friends know together?

dinosaur

____

☐ ______________________
label

2. I have a ring for each finger of both hands. I want to buy 4 more rings. How many rings will I have then?

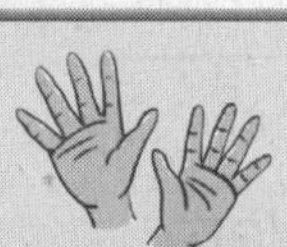
hands

____

☐ ______________________
label

3. Erica had 6 coins in her coin collection. She went to a coin show this week and bought some more. How many coins does she have now?

coin

____

☐ ______________________
label

 Name ______________________

Remembering

Find all of the equations for the 15, 6, 9 Math Mountain.
Draw squiggles under the partners.

1.

15
6 9

6 + 9 = 15  15 = 6 + 9

______  ______

______  ______

______ 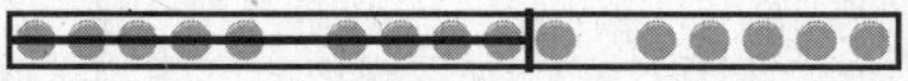 ______

Solve the story problem. **Show your work.**

2. Sofia has 13 pounds of grapes in her basket. She has 6 more pounds than Tony has in his basket. How many pounds of grapes are in Tony's basket?

☐ ______
label

Make a ten or count on to find the partner.

3. 6 + ☐ = 13 17 − 9 = ☐ 5 + ☐ = 14

4. 8 + ☐ = 15 14 − 6 = ☐ 15 − 7 = ☐

5. Measurement Use your centimeter ruler. On a separate piece of paper, draw a rectangle. Find its perimeter.

Name ______

Homework

Solve the story problems.

Show your work.

1. Bessie counted 5 fish, 3 turtles, and some frogs. She counted 14 animals altogether. How many frogs are there?

☐ ______ label

turtle

2. Todd had 4 red blocks and 5 green blocks. Then his sister gave him some blue blocks. Todd has 17 blocks now. How many blue blocks did his sister give him?

☐ ______ label

block

3. There were 15 cups of water in the jug. Jacob poured out 9 cups of water for people at the race to drink. Then his uncle put 7 more cups of water into the jug. How many cups of water are in the jug now?

☐ ______ label

jug

4. Megan had 12 dollars in her pocket. She spent 6 dollars on lunch. Then a friend gave her back the 3 dollars he borrowed yesterday. How much money does Megan have now?

☐ ______ label

lunch

Name ____________________

Targeted Practice

Solve the story problems.

Show your work.

1. Alvin had a dozen pretzels in his bag. For lunch, he ate 9 of them. How many pretzels does Alvin have left?

pretzel

☐ ____________________ label

2. Ed has 10 pairs of shoes in his closet. Alicia has a different pair of shoes for each day of the week. How many pairs of shoes do Ed and Alicia have together?

pair of shoes

☐ ____________________ label

3. Carlos has 8 parakeets as pets. Jeff has a pair of parrots. How many birds do Carlos and Jeff have together?

parakeet

☐ ____________________ label

4. Samuel has 12 horseshoes in his shed. He had to put all new horseshoes on his horse today. How many horseshoes does Samuel have left in his shed?

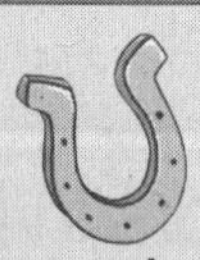

horseshoe

☐ ____________________ label

Name ______________________

Homework

Solve the story problems. | **Show your work.**

1. Jerry ate 6 pieces of pizza. Then he ate 7 more pieces. Vesta ate 9 pieces of pizza. How many fewer pieces of pizza did Vesta eat than Jerry?

☐ ______________ label

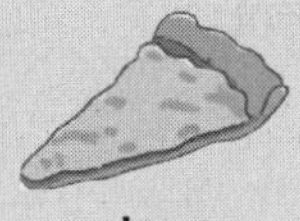

pizza

2. Arnez has 2 angelfish and 5 goldfish. Carmen has 2 angelfish and 6 goldfish. How many more fish does Carmen have than Arnez?

☐ ______________ label

angelfish

3. Chin had 9 shrimp. He ate 3. Then his mother gave him 9 more. How many shrimp does Chin have now?

☐ ______________ label

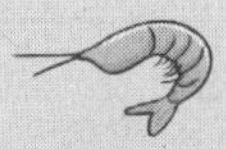

shrimp

4. I bought 3 bananas, 5 apples, and some oranges. Altogether, I bought 15 pieces of fruit. How many oranges did I buy?

☐ ______________ label

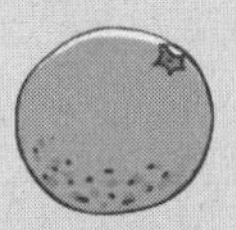

orange

Name ______________________

Remembering

Add or subtract.

1. $\begin{array}{r} 7 \\ +\,8 \\ \hline \end{array}$ $\begin{array}{r} 6 \\ +\,5 \\ \hline \end{array}$ $\begin{array}{r} 9 \\ +\,2 \\ \hline \end{array}$ $\begin{array}{r} 7 \\ +\,5 \\ \hline \end{array}$ $\begin{array}{r} 6 \\ +\,8 \\ \hline \end{array}$ $\begin{array}{r} 3 \\ +\,8 \\ \hline \end{array}$

2. $\begin{array}{r} 13 \\ -\,4 \\ \hline \end{array}$ $\begin{array}{r} 15 \\ -\,8 \\ \hline \end{array}$ $\begin{array}{r} 17 \\ -\,9 \\ \hline \end{array}$ $\begin{array}{r} 16 \\ -\,7 \\ \hline \end{array}$ $\begin{array}{r} 18 \\ -\,9 \\ \hline \end{array}$ $\begin{array}{r} 11 \\ -\,3 \\ \hline \end{array}$

Solve the story problems.

Show your work.

3. Altogether, Adela and Ben have 13 pets. Ben has 6 dogs. Adela has some cats. How many cats does Adela have?

☐ ______________________
label

4. Lonnie planted 16 seeds in his backyard. 4 were sunflower, 6 were tulip, and some were daisy. How many daisy seeds did he plant?

☐ ______________________
label

5. **Measurement** Use your centimeter ruler. On a separate piece of paper, draw a segment 8 centimeters long. Draw all of its partner lengths.

Name ______________________________

Homework

Solve the story problems. | **Show your work.**

1. The school bus will hold 16 children. 3 girls and 6 boys are already on the bus. How many more children can fit on the bus?

☐ ________________
label

school bus

2. Some kites flew in the air. Then 7 of them got caught in trees. Now only 8 kites are flying. How many kites were flying in the beginning?

☐ ________________
label

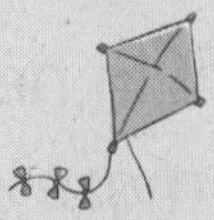
kite

3. Sheldon blew 13 bubbles. 6 of them popped, so he blew 9 more bubbles. How many bubbles are there now?

☐ ________________
label

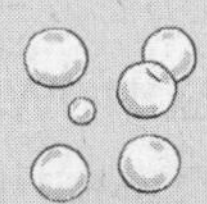
bubbles

4. Explain Your Thinking Explain each step you took to solve problem 3.

____

____

____

Name ______________________________

Targeted Practice

Solve the story problems.

Show your work.

1. Rachel counted 4 cows, 3 goats, and some horses at the farm. She counted 16 animals. How many horses were at the farm?

☐ ______________________
label

cow

2. Allison had 8 dollars in her pocket. Her mother gave her 7 more dollars. Then she spent 5 dollars on lunch. How much money does Allison have now?

☐ ______________________
label

dollar

3. Students made 17 sandwiches for the picnic. They made 3 chicken sandwiches, 6 roast beef sandwiches, and some cheese sandwiches. How many cheese sandwiches did they make?

☐ ______________________
label

sandwich

4. Summarize Explain each step you took to solve problem 3.

____

____

____

Name ____________________

Homework

Cross out any extra information.
Solve the story problems.

Show your work.

1. Edward and his sister read 15 books to their little brother. Edward read 8 of them. His sister ate 2 oranges while Edward read. How many books did his sister read?

☐ ____________________
label

2. Amy had 5 good ideas while taking a walk. Then she had some more good ideas while riding her bike. Altogether she had a total of 12 good ideas. How many good ideas did she have while riding her bike?

☐ ____________________
label

3. Valeria made 13 bracelets. 5 had beads in them. The rest did not. How many bracelets did not have any beads?

☐ ____________________
label

4. Explain Choose one of the three problems. Explain all of the steps you took to solve the problem.

____

____

____

Name ______________________

Remembering

Solve the story problems. **Show your work.**

1. Julio has 17 pairs of shorts. Brian has 9 pairs of shorts. How many more pairs of shorts does Brian need to get to have the same as Julio?

pair of shorts

☐ ______________________ label

2. Shelby has 8 clocks in her house. Theo has 4 clocks in his house. There are 5 clocks in Heather's house. How many clocks do the three of them have altogether?

clock

☐ ______________________ label

Add 3 numbers.

3. 3 + 8 + 2 = ☐ 2 + 3 + 6 = ☐ 2 + 9 + 4 = ☐

4. 7 + 7 + 4 = ☐ 6 + 6 + 4 = ☐ 4 + 7 + 3 = ☐

5. 6 + 2 + 4 = ☐ 9 + 7 + 2 = ☐ 6 + 5 + 3 = ☐

6. Measurement Use your centimeter ruler. On a separate piece of paper, draw a segment 10 centimeters long. Draw all of its partner lengths.

Name ______________________

Homework

Use a centimeter ruler. Find the perimeter of each shape.

1.

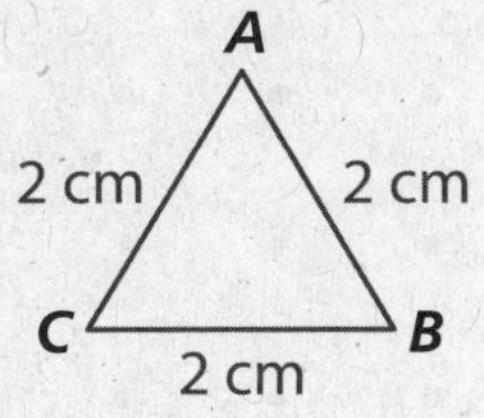

$P =$ ☐ cm

2.

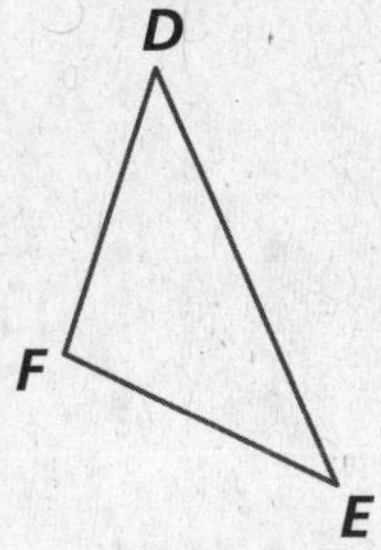

$P =$ ☐ cm

3.

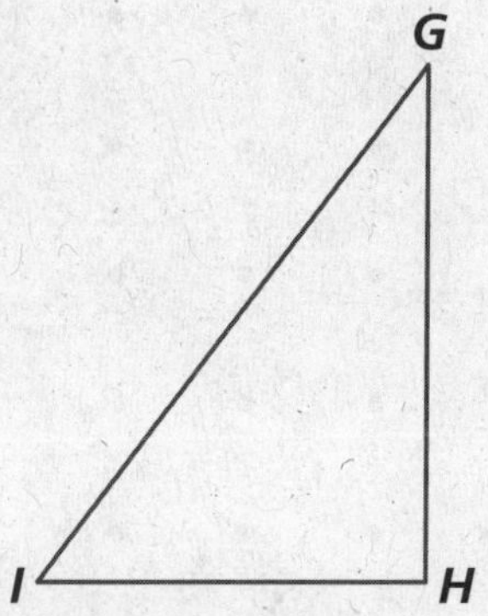

$P =$ ☐ cm

4.

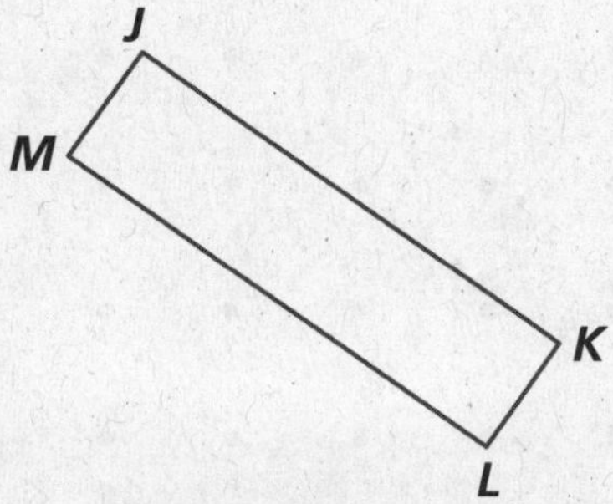

$P =$ ☐ cm

5.

$P =$ ☐ cm

6.

$P =$ ☐ cm

7.

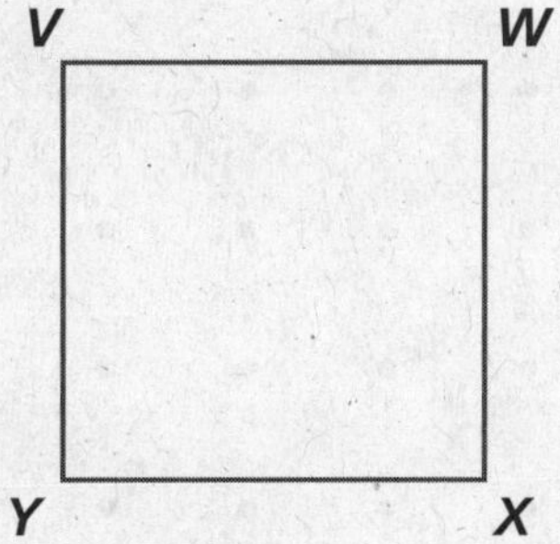

$P =$ ☐ cm

8.

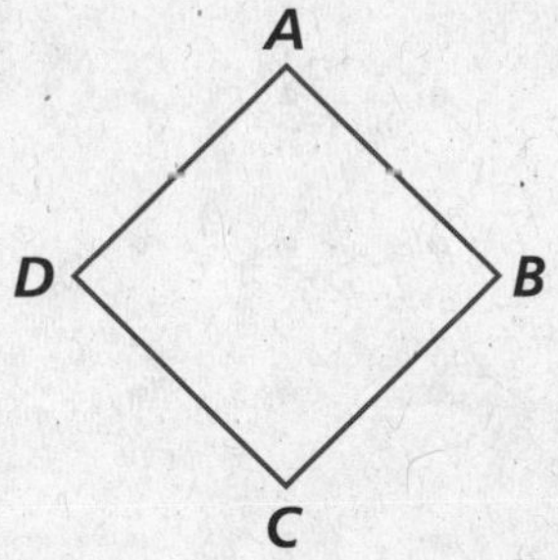

$P =$ ☐ cm

9.

$P =$ ☐ cm

10. On the Back Draw three triangles.

- In the first triangle, all sides have the same length.
- In the second triangle, only two sides have the same length.
- In the third triangle, each side has a different length.

Name ______________________

B–2 **Name** ____________________

Homework

In each row draw three more parallelograms.
The first row is done for you.

1.

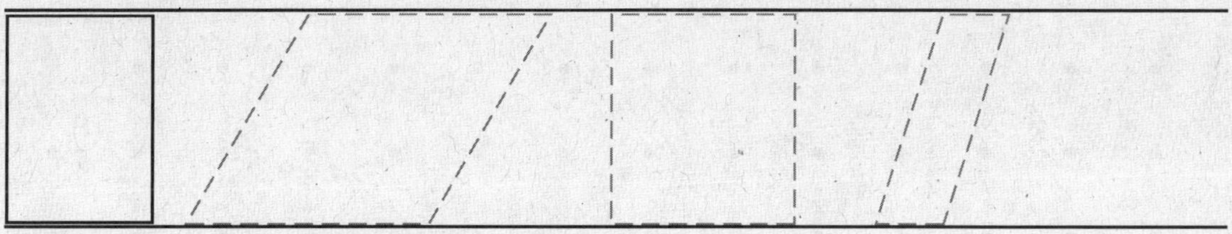

2.

3.

4.

5.

6. On the Back Draw three different parallelograms.

Name

B–3 **Name** ____________________

Homework

Place a check mark beside each word that names the shape.

1.

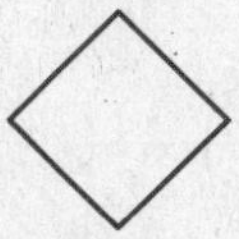

☐ quadrilateral
☐ parallelogram
☐ rectangle
☐ square

2.

☐ quadrilateral
☐ parallelogram
☐ rectangle
☐ square

3.

☐ quadrilateral
☐ parallelogram
☐ rectangle
☐ square

4.

☐ quadrilateral
☐ parallelogram
☐ rectangle
☐ square

5.

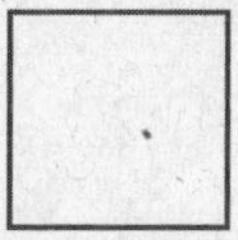

☐ quadrilateral
☐ parallelogram
☐ rectangle
☐ square

6.

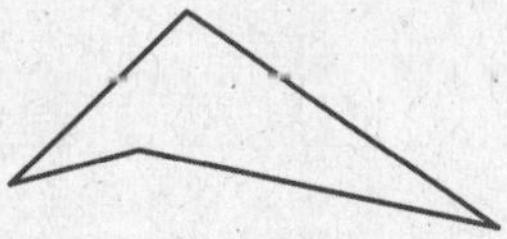

☐ quadrilateral
☐ parallelogram
☐ rectangle
☐ square

7. On the Back Draw three different quadrilaterals that have the same perimeter.

Name

3–1

Name ______________________________

Homework

1. Write the numbers going down to see the tens.

1	11			41			71		
2									92
3						63			
				44			74		
		25							95
					56				
			37						
	18							88	
						69			
10	20			50					100

2. What number comes after 100? ______________

3. What number comes next? ______________

3–1 Name ____________________

Targeted Practice

Solve each story problem.

Show your work.

1. Rama bought 6 onions and 8 carrots. Teresa bought 5 eggplants. How many fewer vegetables did Teresa buy than Rama?

☐ ____________________ label

eggplant

2. There were 18 people at Melvin's party. 7 were girls and the rest were boys. Then 5 boys left. How many boys are still at the party?

☐ ____________________ label

party hat

3. There are 9 computers in the computer lab. 7 girls and 8 boys want to use the computers. How many children do not get to use a computer?

☐ ____________________ label

computer

4. Melissa has 4 red feathers, 5 purple feathers, and some yellow feathers in her hat. She has 16 feathers in total. How many feathers are yellow?

☐ ____________________ label

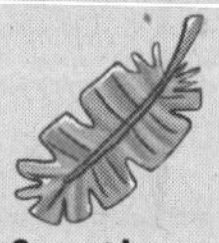
feather

Name ______________________

Homework

Add.

1. 50 + 40 = ____ 80 + 10 = ____ 60 + 20 = ____

   5 + 4 = ____ 8 + 1 = ____ 6 + 2 = ____

2. 10 + 70 = ____ 30 + 70 = ____ 40 + 30 = ____

   1 + 7 = ____ 3 + 7 = ____ 4 + 3 = ____

3. 30 + 60 = ____ 20 + 80 = ____ 50 + 40 = ____

   3 + 6 = ____ 2 + 8 = ____ 5 + 4 = ____

4. 50 + 30 = ____ 70 + 20 = ____ 40 + 60 = ____

   5 + 3 = ____ 7 + 2 = ____ 4 + 6 = ____

5. 90 + 10 = ____ 50 + 20 = ____ 20 + 30 = ____

   9 + 1 = ____ 5 + 2 = ____ 2 + 3 = ____

6. 30 + 10 = ____ 50 + 30 = ____ 40 + 20 = ____

   3 + 1 = ____ 5 + 3 = ____ 4 + 2 = ____

Name ____________________

Remembering

Fill in the Venn diagram to show some things that belong together.

1.

pets
____
Group Name

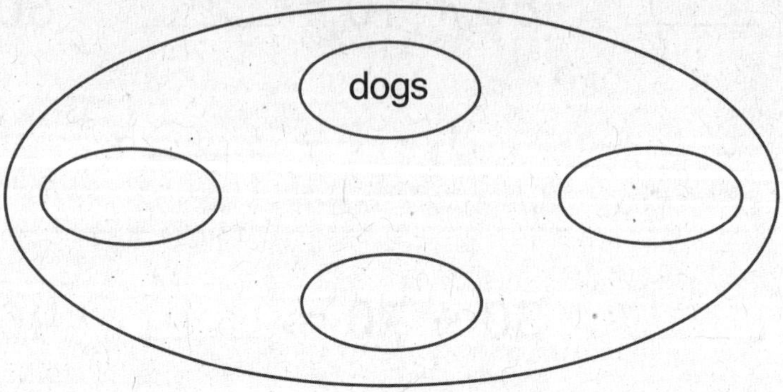

Write the Math Mountain equations. Draw squiggles under the partners.

2.

12
8 4

8 + 4 = 12 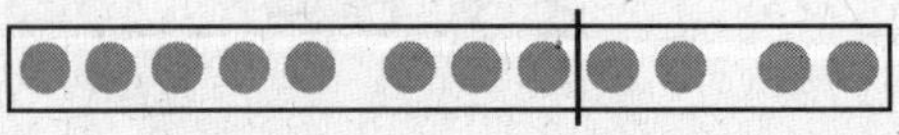 12 = 8 + 4

__________ 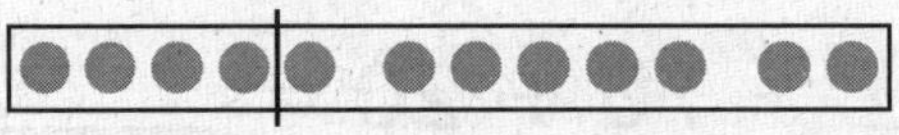 __________

__________ 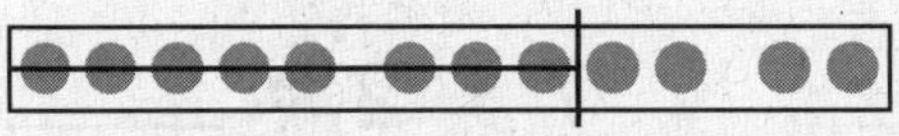 __________

__________  __________

Add or subtract.

3. 5 + 0 = ______ 10 – 0 = ______ 2 – 1 = ______

4. 2 + 1 = ______ 4 – 0 = ______ 9 + 1 = ______

5. Measurement On a separate piece of paper, draw 3 shapes with the same perimeter.

3–3

Name ______________________

Homework

Draw these numbers using hundred boxes, ten sticks, and circles. Then write the hundreds, tens, and ones.

1.	2.	3.

1. 176

100 + 70 + 6

2. 143

____ + ____ + ____

3. 184

____ + ____ + ____

What numbers are shown here?

H = Hundreds, T = Tens, O = Ones

4.

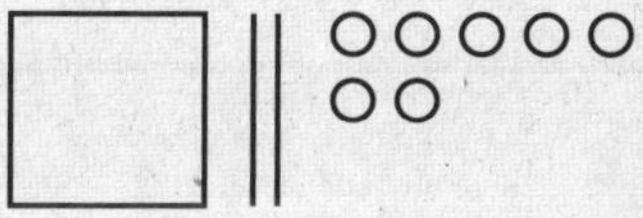

1 H 2 T 7 O

127 = 100 + 20 + 7

5.

____ H ____ T ____ O

____ = ____ + ____ + ____

6.

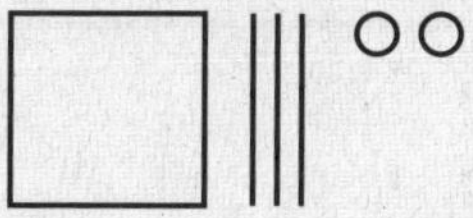

____ H ____ T ____ O

____ = ____ + ____ + ____

7.

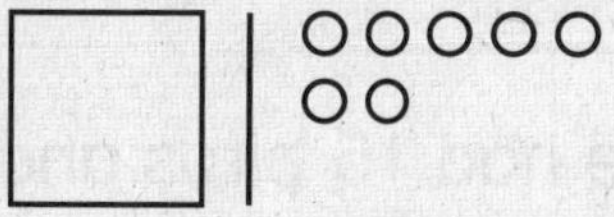

____ H ____ T ____ O

____ = ____ + ____ + ____

Name ______________________________

Targeted Practice

Solve each story problem. **Show your work.**

1. Erin bought 4 red pens, 5 blue pens, and some black pens. She bought a total of 15 pens. How many black pens did Erin buy?

☐ ______________________
label

pen

2. There are 18 chairs in the classroom. 7 boys and 6 girls need to sit in the classroom. How many chairs will not be used?

☐ ______________________
label

chair

3. Nicole made 20 muffins. 8 were blueberry muffins, and the rest were apple muffins. Then she gave away 5 apple muffins. How many apple muffins does she have now?

☐ ______________________
label

muffin

4. The pet store had 15 birds and some rabbits. They had 6 fewer rabbits than birds. Today they sold 3 rabbits. How many rabbits does the store have left?

☐ ______________________
label

rabbit

Name ____________________

Homework

Add.

1. 25 + 7 = ____
2. 24 + 3 = ____
3. 73 + 3 = ____
4. 37 + 6 = ____
5. 59 + 5 = ____
6. 69 + 4 = ____
7. 26 + 8 = ____
8. 67 + 8 = ____
9. 37 + 2 = ____
10. 33 + 7 = ____
11. 56 + 6 = ____
12. 47 + 5 = ____

---

13. 40 + 60 = ____   20 + 80 = ____   30 + 30 = ____

 4 + 6 = ____   2 + 8 = ____   3 + 3 = ____

---

14. 50 + 20 = ____   70 + 20 = ____   40 + 80 = ____

 5 + 2 = ____   7 + 2 = ____   4 + 8 = ____

---

15. 50 + 40 = ____   60 + 20 = ____   20 + 30 = ____

 5 + 4 = ____   6 + 2 = ____   2 + 3 = ____

---

16. 30 + 60 = ____   10 + 50 = ____   40 + 40 = ____

 3 + 6 = ____   1 + 5 = ____   4 + 4 = ____

 Name ____________________

Remembering

Add the 3 numbers.

1. 3 + 2 + 6 = ____
2. 6 + 3 + 3 = ____
3. 7 + 3 + 2 = ____
4. 3 + 5 + 6 = ____
5. 9 + 4 + 2 = ____
6. 5 + 6 + 3 = ____
7. 5 + 8 + 5 = ____
8. 8 + 3 + 7 = ____
9. 3 + 9 + 6 = ____
10. 7 + 3 + 7 = ____
11. 9 + 3 + 3 = ____
12. 8 + 5 + 4 = ____

Complete the Partner Houses.

13.

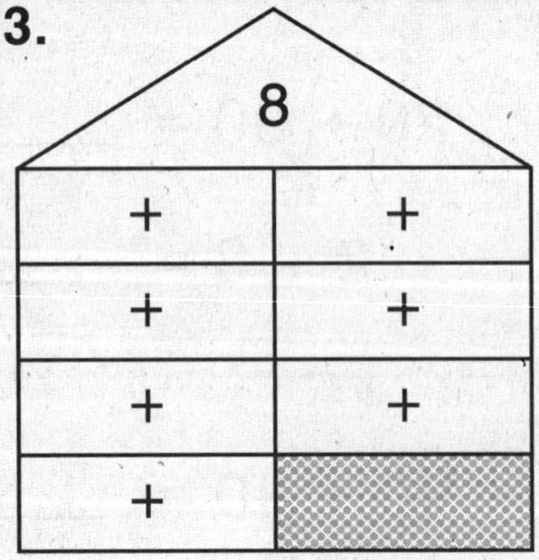

14.

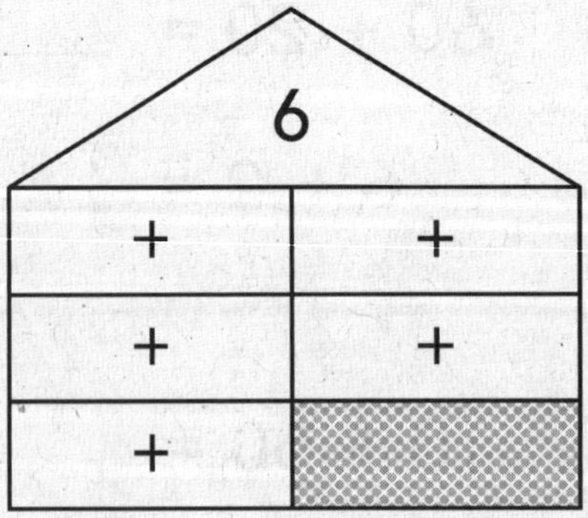

15.

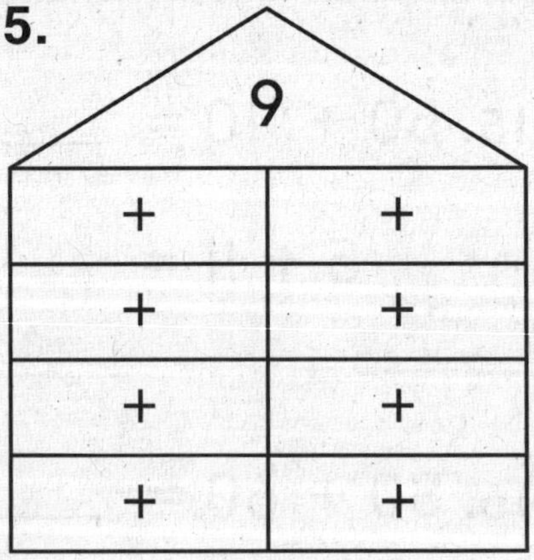

16. **Measurement** On a separate piece of paper, draw 3 shapes with the same perimeter.

3–5

Name ______________________

Homework

Group the 10-partners. The first one is done for you.

1. 3 + 7 = 10

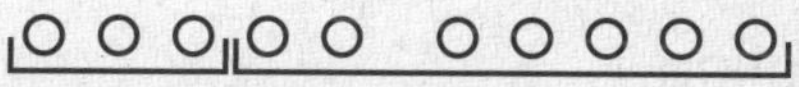

2. 9 + 1 = 10

3. 4 + 6 = 10

Group the 100-partners. The first one is done for you.

4. 30 + 70 = 100

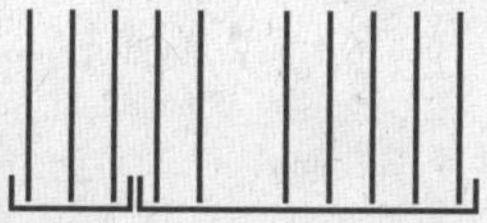

5. 90 + 10 = 100

6. 40 + 60 = 100

Add.

7. 80 + 60 = ____ 60 + 90 = ____ 60 + 70 = ____

8 + 6 = ____ 6 + 9 = ____ 6 + 7 = ____

8. 70 + 50 = ____ 30 + 90 = ____ 90 + 60 = ____

7 + 5 = ____ 3 + 9 = ____ 9 + 6 = ____

9. 40 + 90 = ____ 90 + 80 = ____ 80 + 50 = ____

4 + 9 = ____ 9 + 8 = ____ 8 + 5 = ____

Name ______________________________

Targeted Practice

Cross out the extra information.
Solve the story problems.

Show your work.

---

1. There were 6 trains and 2 buses at Main Street Station. 9 more buses and 4 more trains just arrived. How many buses are at the station now?

☐ ____________________
label

bus station

---

2. The pet store had 12 kittens and 11 puppies. Today they sold 3 puppies. How many puppies does the pet store still have?

☐ ____________________
label

kitten

---

3. The farmer has 8 cows and 6 turkeys. He just bought 7 more turkeys. How many turkeys does the farmer have now?

☐ ____________________
label

turkey

---

4. Jane checked out 9 nature books and 7 adventure books from the library. Then she returned 5 nature books. How many nature books does she still have?

☐ ____________________
label

nature book

3–6 Name

Homework

Solve each story problem.

1. Mina picked 63 flowers from her garden. She can put 10 flowers in each vase. How many vases will be filled up? How many extra flowers will she have?

☐ vases ☐ extra flowers

2. Luisa has 85 coupons. She can trade in 10 of them for a toy. How many toys can Luisa get for her coupons? How many coupons will she have left over?

☐ toys ☐ coupons left over

3. Mustafa wants to buy books that cost 10 dollars each. He has 45 dollars. How many books can he buy? How many dollars will he have left over?

☐ books ☐ dollars left over

4. The track team has 72 water bottles. They pack them 10 to a box. How many boxes can they fill with bottles? How many water bottles will be left over?

☐ boxes ☐ water bottles left over

Name ______________________________

Remembering

What numbers are shown here?

H = Hundreds, T = Tens, O = Ones

1. 

____ H ____ T ____ O

____ = ____ + ____ + ____

2. 

____ H ____ T ____ O

____ = ____ + ____ + ____

3. 

____ H ____ T ____ O

____ = ____ + ____ + ____

4. 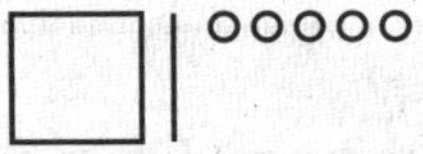

____ H ____ T ____ O

____ = ____ + ____ + ____

Solve each story problem.

Show your work.

5. Lee bought 7 pencils on Friday. On Saturday she bought 3 erasers and 4 pencils. How many pencils did she buy altogether on those two days?

☐ ______________________
label

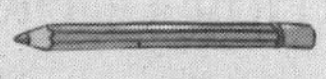

pencil

6. Corey saw 5 ducks. James saw 13 ducks. How many fewer ducks did Corey see than James?

☐ ______________________
label

duck

7. **Measurement** On a separate piece of paper, draw 3 shapes with the same perimeter.

Name ______

Homework

Add ones, tens, or a hundred.

1. 9 + 8 = ____ 7 + 7 = ____ 9 + 5 = ____

90 + 80 = ____ 70 + 70 = ____ 90 + 50 = ____

2. 6 + 8 = ____ 8 + 3 = ____ 9 + 7 = ____

60 + 80 = ____ 80 + 30 = ____ 90 + 70 = ____

3. 7 + 5 = ____ 6 + 9 = ____ 8 + 8 = ____

70 + 50 = ____ 60 + 90 = ____ 80 + 80 = ____

4. 8 + 7 = ____ 6 + 5 = ____ 9 + 4 = ____

80 + 70 = ____ 60 + 50 = ____ 90 + 40 = ____

5. 100 + 48 = ____ **6.** 21 + 100 = ____ **7.** 100 + 2 = ____

10 + 48 = ____ 21 + 10 = ____ 10 + 2 = ____

1 + 48 = ____ 21 + 1 = ____ 1 + 2 = ____

Name

Targeted Practice

Add.

1. $\begin{array}{r} 28 \\ +\ 19 \\ \hline \end{array}$ $\begin{array}{r} 52 \\ +\ 33 \\ \hline \end{array}$ $\begin{array}{r} 59 \\ +\ 27 \\ \hline \end{array}$

2. $\begin{array}{r} 45 \\ +\ 16 \\ \hline \end{array}$ $\begin{array}{r} 54 \\ +\ 37 \\ \hline \end{array}$ $\begin{array}{r} 38 \\ +\ 21 \\ \hline \end{array}$

3. $\begin{array}{r} 25 \\ +\ 62 \\ \hline \end{array}$ $\begin{array}{r} 23 \\ +\ 48 \\ \hline \end{array}$ $\begin{array}{r} 55 \\ +\ 35 \\ \hline \end{array}$

4. $\begin{array}{r} 77 \\ +\ 14 \\ \hline \end{array}$ $\begin{array}{r} 56 \\ +\ 29 \\ \hline \end{array}$ $\begin{array}{r} 41 \\ +\ 38 \\ \hline \end{array}$

Name

Homework

Solve the story problems. **Show your work.**

1. Kivy made 34 baskets. Her father made 58 baskets. How many baskets did they make in all?

☐ ________
label

2. Glen printed 67 posters yesterday and 86 more today. How many posters did he print in total?

☐ ________
label

Add.

3. $39 + 44$ $67 + 56$ $47 + 98$

4. $48 + 33$ $85 + 68$ $94 + 57$

 Name

Remembering

Add.

1. 7 + 3 = ____ 6 + 9 = ____ 8 + 3 = ____

70 + 30 = ____ 60 + 90 = ____ 80 + 30 = ____

2. 6 + 6 = ____ 4 + 8 = ____ 9 + 9 = ____

60 + 60 = ____ 40 + 80 = ____ 90 + 90 = ____

3. 6 + 4 = ____ 5 + 2 = ____ 100 + 14 = ____

60 + 40 = ____ 50 + 20 = ____ 10 + 14 = ____

1 + 14 = ____

Draw these numbers using boxes, sticks, and circles.
Then write the hundreds, tens, and ones.

4. 127

100 + 20 + 7

5. 109

____ + ____ + ____

6. 133

____ + ____ + ____

7. **Measurement** On a separate piece of paper, draw 3 shapes with the same perimeter.

Name ______________________________

Homework

```
  86    or    86
+ 57        + 57
 130         143
+ 13
 143
```

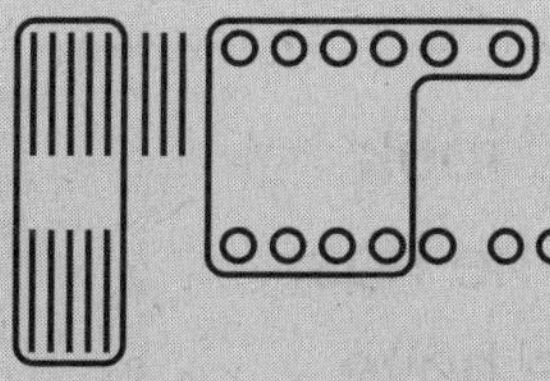

130 + 13 = 143

Add. Use any method.

1. 97 + 45	54 + 39	35 + 47
2. 56 + 77	76 + 88	86 + 65
3. 47 + 73	87 + 49	57 + 48

3-10 **Name** ______________________

Targeted Practice

Solve each story problem. **Show your work.**

1. Greg had some library books. He took 8 books back to the library. Now he has 8 books. How many books did he have in the beginning?

☐ ______________________
label

library

2. Asha drew some pictures. Then she drew 5 more pictures. Now she has 14 pictures. How many did she draw first?

☐ ______________________
label

picture

3. Sam's mom gave him some crackers. He ate 9 crackers. He has 6 crackers left. How many crackers did his mom give him?

☐ ______________________
label

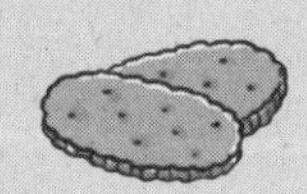

crackers

4. Some children were playing at the park. 7 children came. There are 14 children playing at the park now. How many children were playing at the park to start?

☐ ______________________
label

park

Name ______

Homework

$$\begin{array}{r} 75 \\ +\ 49 \\ \hline 110 \\ +\ 14 \\ \hline 124 \end{array} \quad \text{or} \quad \begin{array}{r} 75 \\ +\ 49 \\ \hline 124 \end{array}$$

$110 + 14 = 124$

Add. Use any method.

1. $\begin{array}{r} 83 \\ +\ 79 \\ \hline \end{array}$ $\begin{array}{r} 65 \\ +\ 47 \\ \hline \end{array}$ $\begin{array}{r} 78 \\ +\ 34 \\ \hline \end{array}$

2. $\begin{array}{r} 74 \\ +\ 99 \\ \hline \end{array}$ $\begin{array}{r} 48 \\ +\ 87 \\ \hline \end{array}$ $\begin{array}{r} 92 \\ +\ 59 \\ \hline \end{array}$

3. $\begin{array}{r} 63 \\ +\ 77 \\ \hline \end{array}$ $\begin{array}{r} 75 \\ +\ 48 \\ \hline \end{array}$ $\begin{array}{r} 86 \\ +\ 32 \\ \hline \end{array}$

Name ______________________

Remembering

Solve the story problems.

Show your work.

1. The Denny Tree Farm has 84 pine trees. Baker's Acres has 37 pine trees. How many pine trees do both places have?

☐ ______________________
label

pine tree

2. Lin found some shells. Lee found 9 more shells. They now have 17 shells. How many shells did Lin find?

☐ ______________________
label

shell

3. The jewelry store has 48 watches on sale. The pharmacy next door has 23 watches on sale. How many watches do the two stores have to sell in all?

☐ ______________________
label

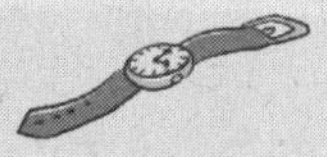
watch

4. The Day Care Center has 29 teddy bears. They just ordered 75 more. How many teddy bears will the Day Care Center have when the order comes in?

☐ ______________________
label

teddy bear

5. Measurement On a separate piece of paper, draw 3 shapes with the same perimeter.

3–12

Name

Homework

Be the helper. Is the answer OK? Write *yes* or *no*.
If *no*, fix the mistakes and write the correct answer.

43 + 28 = 71 (regrouping mark: 1)	OK? Yes	45 + 23 = 78 (regrouping mark: 1)	OK? No → 45 + 23 = ~~78~~ 68 (regrouping mark crossed out)

1. 27 + 45 = 72 (regrouping mark: 1) OK? ☐

2. 68 + 26 = 84 (regrouping mark: 1) OK? ☐

3. 32 + 29 = 511 OK? ☐

4. 16 + 67 = 91 (regrouping mark: 2) OK? ☐

5. 59 + 25 = 74 OK? ☐

6. 51 + 44 = 95 OK? ☐

7. 85 + 56 = 141 (regrouping mark: 1) OK? ☐

8. 58 + 99 = 147 OK? ☐

9. 73 + 82 = 165 (regrouping mark: 1) OK? ☐

Name ____________________

Targeted Practice

Add. Use any method.

1. $\begin{array}{r} 42 \\ +\ 74 \\ \hline \end{array}$ $\begin{array}{r} 88 \\ +\ 91 \\ \hline \end{array}$ $\begin{array}{r} 61 \\ +\ 73 \\ \hline \end{array}$

2. $\begin{array}{r} 75 \\ +\ 33 \\ \hline \end{array}$ $\begin{array}{r} 42 \\ +\ 97 \\ \hline \end{array}$ $\begin{array}{r} 27 \\ +\ 71 \\ \hline \end{array}$

3. $\begin{array}{r} 95 \\ +\ 61 \\ \hline \end{array}$ $\begin{array}{r} 22 \\ +\ 93 \\ \hline \end{array}$ $\begin{array}{r} 81 \\ +\ 71 \\ \hline \end{array}$

4. $\begin{array}{r} 36 \\ +\ 92 \\ \hline \end{array}$ $\begin{array}{r} 82 \\ +\ 75 \\ \hline \end{array}$ $\begin{array}{r} 54 \\ +\ 73 \\ \hline \end{array}$

3–13 Name ______________________

Homework

Solve each story problem.

1. Here is the path Fluffy took on her walk today. How many yards did she walk?

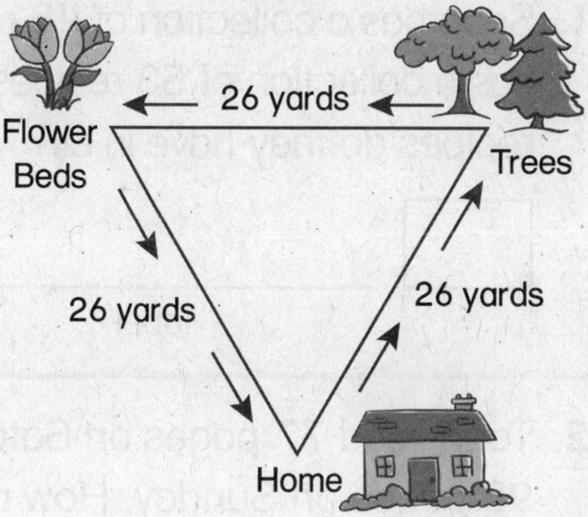

☐ ______________
label

2. Colin wants to decorate a picture frame with gold ribbon. How long should the ribbon be if he wants to outline the whole frame?

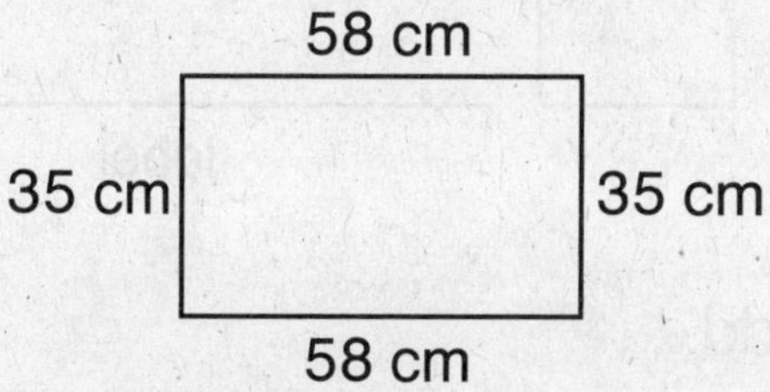

☐ ______________
label

3. Here is a top view drawing of the new sandbox for the park. Each side is 16 feet long. A wooden seat runs along the perimeter. How long is the seat?

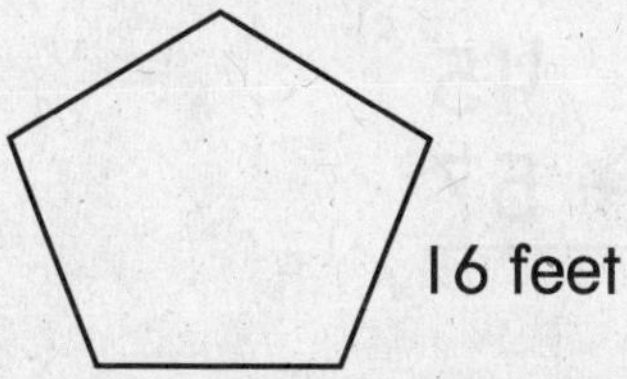

☐ ______________
label

Name ______________________________

Remembering

Solve each story problem. **Show your work.**

1. Sean has a collection of 48 recipes. Hannah has a collection of 53 recipes. How many recipes do they have in all?

recipes

☐ ______________________
label

2. Todd read 77 pages on Saturday. He read 93 pages on Sunday. How many pages did he read in the two days?

pages

☐ ______________________
label

Add.

3.

$$\begin{array}{r} 64 \\ +\ 87 \\ \hline \end{array} \qquad \begin{array}{r} 19 \\ +\ 78 \\ \hline \end{array} \qquad \begin{array}{r} 13 \\ +\ 79 \\ \hline \end{array}$$

4.

$$\begin{array}{r} 45 \\ +\ 57 \\ \hline \end{array} \qquad \begin{array}{r} 26 \\ +\ 97 \\ \hline \end{array} \qquad \begin{array}{r} 86 \\ +\ 59 \\ \hline \end{array}$$

5. Measurement On a separate piece of paper, draw 3 shapes with the same perimeter.

Name ______________________

Homework

Here are some more fruits and vegetables from the Farm Stand. Answer the questions below. Then draw the money amount. The first one is done for you.

Apples 79¢	Eggplant 96¢	Pears 58¢	Green Onions 67¢	Oranges 85¢
	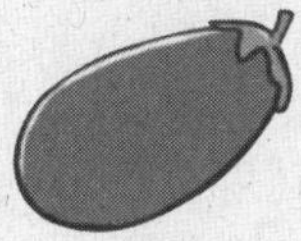		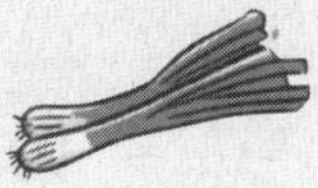	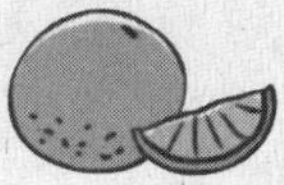

How much would you spend if you wanted to buy

1. apples and oranges? 164 ¢   [1 dollar] (10¢) (10¢) (10¢) (10¢) (10¢) (10¢) (1¢) (1¢) (1¢) (1¢)

2. apples and green onions? ______ ¢

3. pears and green onions? ______ ¢

4. pears and apples? ______ ¢

5. eggplant and oranges? ______ ¢

3–14 Name ____________________

Targeted Practice

Under the coins write the total amount of money so far.
The first one is done for you.

1. 10¢ 10¢ 5¢ 5¢ 1¢ 1¢

10¢ 20¢ 25¢ 30¢ 31¢ 32¢

2. 10¢ 10¢ 10¢ 10¢ 10¢ 1¢

____ ____ ____ ____ ____ ____

3. 10¢ 5¢ 5¢ 5¢ 1¢ 1¢ 1¢

____ ____ ____ ____ ____ ____ ____

4. 10¢ 5¢ 1¢ 1¢ 1¢ 1¢

____ ____ ____ ____ ____ ____

5. Draw the coins you could use to show 85¢.
Use (D), (N), and (P).

Name ______________________________

Homework

Here are some more foods from the snack bar. Answer the questions below. Then draw the money amounts using dollars, dimes, nickels, and pennies.

Hot Dog 87¢	Peach 76¢	Sandwich 98¢	Corn on the Cob 65¢	Watermelon 59¢

How much would you spend if you wanted to buy

1. a hot dog and corn on the cob? ______________ ¢

2. a sandwich and a peach? ______________ ¢

3. watermelon and a hot dog? ______________ ¢

4. a sandwich and watermelon? ______________ ¢

5. **Problem Solving** Ivan has 6 coins. The value of his coins is 37¢. Three of his coins are dimes. What are the other 3 coins?

____

Name ______________________________

Remembering

Solve each story problem. **Show your work.**

1. There are 53 green peppers in the vegetable bin. There are 59 yellow peppers in the vegetable bin. How many green and yellow peppers are there in all?

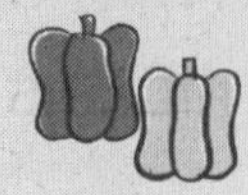

☐ ____________ label

2. Seth found some rocks in a field. Mandy found 5 more rocks. There are now 13 rocks. How many rocks did Seth find?

☐ ____________ label

3. Ted's Trucking Company had 84 trucks. They just bought 28 new trucks. How many trucks do they have now?

☐ ____________ label

Add.

4. $\begin{array}{r} 49 \\ +\ 85 \\ \hline \end{array}$ $\quad$ $\begin{array}{r} 93 \\ +\ 56 \\ \hline \end{array}$ $\quad$ $\begin{array}{r} 61 \\ +\ 39 \\ \hline \end{array}$

5. Measurement On a separate piece of paper, draw 3 shapes with the same perimeter.

3–16

Homework

Name ____________________

Complete the number sequence. Write the rule.

1. 12, 14, 16, ____, ____, ____, ____ Rule: n + 2

2. 25, 30, 35, ____, ____, ____, ____ Rule: n ____

3. 49, 52, 55, ____, ____, ____, ____ Rule: n ____

4. 80, 90, 100, ____, ____, ____, ____ Rule: n ____

5. 46, 56, 66, ____, ____, ____, ____ Rule: n ____

6. 58, 56, 54, ____, ____, ____, ____ Rule: n − 2

7. 39, 36, 33, ____, ____, ____, ____ Rule: n ____

8. 48, 42, 36, ____, ____, ____, ____ Rule: n ____

9. 70, 65, 60, ____, ____, ____, ____ Rule: n ____

10. 126, 130, 134, ____, ____, ____, ____ Rule: n ____

11. 135, 140, 145, ____, ____, ____, ____ Rule: n ____

12. **Explain Your Thinking** Which takes less time? Explain.
    - Skip count by 2s from 2 to 100.
    - Skip count by 5s from 5 to 100.

____

____

____

Name ______

Targeted Practice

Complete the number sequence. Write the rule.

1. 15, 21, 27, ______, ______, ______ Rule: *n* + 6

2. 39, 35, 31, ______, ______, ______ Rule: *n* ______

3. 29, 34, 39, ______, ______, ______ Rule: *n* ______

4. 43, 39, 35, ______, ______, ______ Rule: *n* ______

5. 66, 69, 72, ______, ______, ______ Rule: *n* ______

6. 43, 35, 27, ______, ______, ______ Rule: *n* ______

7. 84, 86, 88, ______, ______, ______ Rule: *n* ______

8. 52, 46, 40, ______, ______, ______ Rule: *n* ______

9. 21, 29, 37, ______, ______, ______ Rule: *n* ______

10. 90, 87, 84, ______, ______, ______ Rule: *n* ______

11. 11, 17, 23, ______, ______, ______ Rule: *n* ______

12. 49, 56, 63, ______, ______, ______ Rule: *n* ______

13. 37, 48, 59, ______, ______, ______ Rule: *n* ______

14. 84, 75, 66, ______, ______, ______ Rule: *n* ______

Name ____________________

Homework

Solve each story problem.

Show your work.

1. The theater can hold 100 people. We sold 62 tickets to the play. How many more tickets do we have to sell to fill the theater?

theater

☐ ____________________ label

2. My orchard has 82 trees in it. 47 are lime trees. The rest are lemon trees. How many lemon trees do I have?

orchard

☐ ____________________ label

3. There are 75 seats on the airplane. 41 of them are near a window. The rest are not. How many seats are not near a window?

window

☐ ____________________ label

4. The gift store sold 93 plant and animal key chains. 48 were plant key chains. How many were animal key chains?

key chain

☐ ____________________ label

5. Find the unknown partner.

100: 68 and ☐

100: 19 and ☐

93: 49 and ☐

54: 18 and ☐

Name ______________________________

Remembering

Here are some more foods from the snack bar. Answer the questions below. Then draw the money amount.

Hot Dog 87¢	Grapes 78¢	Yogurt 68¢	Popcorn 45¢	Fruit Juice 79¢

How much would you spend if you wanted to buy

1. fruit juice and a hot dog? ______________ ¢

2. yogurt and popcorn? ______________ ¢

Solve the story problem. **Show your work.**

3. Dora caught 4 butterflies in her net. Joel caught some more butterflies. Now there are 13 butterflies. How many butterflies did Joel catch?

☐ ____________________
label

butterflies

4. Measurement On a separate piece of paper, draw 3 shapes with the same perimeter.

Name ____________________

Homework

Write the time in two different ways.

1.

_______ o'clock

2.

_______ o'clock

3.

_______ o'clock

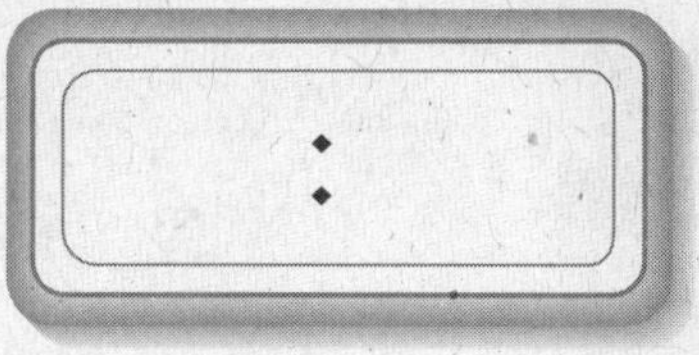

Draw the hands on each analog clock and write the time on each digital clock below.

4.

1 o'clock

5.

6 o'clock

6.

12 o'clock

For each activity, ring the appropriate time.

7. Eat an afternoon snack.

3:00 A.M. 2:00 P.M. 6:00 P.M.

8. Go to a movie at night.

8:00 A.M. 12:00 NOON 7:00 P.M.

9. On the Back Draw a picture of what you might do at 7:00 P.M. Draw a clock face with hands to show the time.

Name

C–2 Name ______________________________

Homework

Write the time on the digital clocks.

1.

2.

3.

4.

Draw hands on the analog clocks to show the time.

5.

6.

7.

8.

Fill in the answers.

9. 3 fives = ________ **10.** 7 fives = ________ **11.** 4 fives = ________

12. 8 fives = ________ **13.** 2 fives = ________ **14.** 5 fives = ________

15. 1 five = ________ **16.** 6 fives = ________ **17.** 9 fives = ________

18. On the Back Draw a picture of what you were doing at 8:15 this morning. Draw an analog clock showing the time.

Name

C–3

Homework

Name ______________________________

Fill in the missing numbers on the clock faces below.
Draw hands on each clock to show the time.

1.

2.

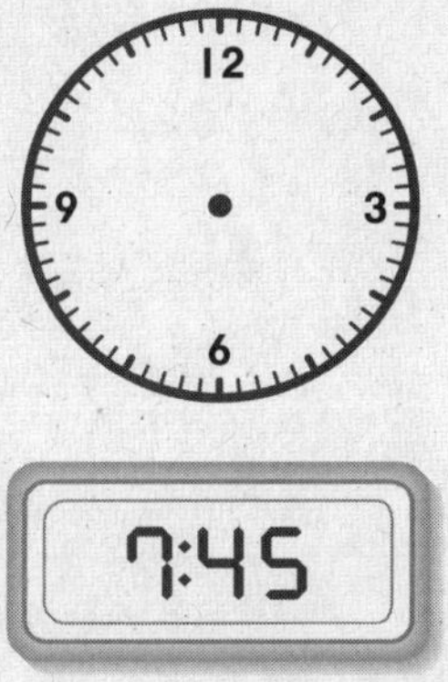

3.

4.

Write the time on each digital clock.

5.

6.

7.

8.

9. Write the time.

______ minutes before ______

______ minutes after ______

10. On the Back Draw a picture of what you might do at 7:15 A.M. and 7:15 P.M. Draw an analog clock showing the time for each activity.

Name ______________________

C-4

Name ____________________

Homework

Write the start and end times. Then find how much time passed.

Start Time	End Time	How Long Did It Take?
1.  ________ P.M.	 ________ P.M.	________ hour(s)
2.  ________ A.M.	 ________ A.M.	________ hour(s)
3.  ________ A.M.	 ________ A.M.	________ hour(s)

For the activity, ring the unit of time you would use.

4. Bake cookies in an oven.

days seconds minutes months

5. On the Back Make a timetable showing how you spend the hours from the time you get home from school to the time you go to sleep.

Name

C–5

Homework

Name ______________________________

Use the calendar to answer questions 1 and 2.

January

S	M	T	W	TH	F	S
1	2	3	4	5	6	7
8	9	10	11	12	13	14
15	16	17	18	19	20	21
22	23	24	25	26	27	28
29	30	31				

February

S	M	T	W	TH	F	S
			1	2	3	4
5	6	7	8	9	10	11
12	13	14	15	16	17	18
19	20	21	22	23	24	25
26	27	28				

March

S	M	T	W	TH	F	S
			1	2	3	4
5	6	7	8	9	10	11
12	13	14	15	16	17	18
19	20	21	22	23	24	25
26	27	28	29	30	31	

April

S	M	T	W	TH	F	S
						1
2	3	4	5	6	7	8
9	10	11	12	13	14	15
16	17	18	19	20	21	22
23	24	25	26	27	28	29
30						

May

S	M	T	W	TH	F	S
	1	2	3	4	5	6
7	8	9	10	11	12	13
14	15	16	17	18	19	20
21	22	23	24	25	26	27
28	29	30	31			

June

S	M	T	W	TH	F	S
				1	2	3
4	5	6	7	8	9	10
11	12	13	14	15	16	17
18	19	20	21	22	23	24
25	26	27	28	29	30	

July

S	M	T	W	TH	F	S
						1
2	3	4	5	6	7	8
9	10	11	12	13	14	15
16	17	18	19	20	21	22
23	24	25	26	27	28	29
30	31					

August

S	M	T	W	TH	F	S
		1	2	3	4	5
6	7	8	9	10	11	12
13	14	15	16	17	18	19
20	21	22	23	24	25	26
27	28	29	30	31		

September

S	M	T	W	TH	F	S
					1	2
3	4	5	6	7	8	9
10	11	12	13	14	15	16
17	18	19	20	21	22	23
24	25	26	27	28	29	30

October

S	M	T	W	TH	F	S
1	2	3	4	5	6	7
8	9	10	11	12	13	14
15	16	17	18	19	20	21
22	23	24	25	26	27	28
29	30	31				

November

S	M	T	W	TH	F	S
			1	2	3	4
5	6	7	8	9	10	11
12	13	14	15	16	17	18
19	20	21	22	23	24	25
26	27	28	29	30		

December

S	M	T	W	TH	F	S
					1	2
3	4	5	6	7	8	9
10	11	12	13	14	15	16
17	18	19	20	21	22	23
24	25	26	27	28	29	30
31						

1. Which month immediately follows February?

____

2. What day of the week does November begin with?

____

Complete the table to solve the problem.

3. So Lum travels 8 miles each school day. How far does she travel in one school week?

______________________ miles

Days	**1**	**2**	**3**	**4**	**5**
Distance (miles)					

4. On the Back Write and solve your own problem using the calendar above.

Name

Houghton Mifflin

Math Expressions

Volume 2

Homework and Remembering

Developed by
The Children's Math Worlds Research Project

PROJECT DIRECTOR AND AUTHOR

Dr. Karen C. Fuson

This material is based upon work supported by the
National Science Foundation
under Grant Numbers
ESI-9816320, REC-9806020, and RED-935373.

Any opinions, findings, and conclusions or recommendations expressed in this material are those of the author and do not necessarily reflect the views of the National Science Foundation.

HOUGHTON MIFFLIN BOSTON

Teacher Reviewers

Kindergarten
Patricia Stroh Sugiyama
Wilmette, Illinois

Barbara Wahle
Evanston, Illinois

Grade 1
Sandra Budson
Newton, Massachusetts

Janet Pecci
Chicago, Illinois

Megan Rees
Chicago, Illinois

Grade 2
Molly Dunn
Danvers, Massachusetts

Agnes Lesnick
Hillside, Illinois

Rita Soto
Chicago, Illinois

Grade 3
Jane Curran
Honesdale, Pennsylvania

Sandra Tucker
Chicago, Illinois

Grade 4
Sara Stoneberg Llibre
Chicago, Illinois

Sheri Roedel
Chicago, Illinois

Grade 5
Todd Atler
Chicago, Illinois

Leah Barry
Norfolk, Massachusetts

Credits

Cover art: (tiger) © Juniors Bildarchiv/Alamy Images. (whale) © Francois Gohier/Photo Researchers, Inc. (grass) © Corel Stock Photo Library. (tape) © Eyewire.

Illustrative art: Robin Boyer/Deborah Wolfe, LTD
Technical art: Nesbitt Graphics, Inc.
Photos: Nesbitt Graphics, Inc.

Printed in the U.S.A.

ISBN-13: 978-0-618-64113-0
ISBN-10: 0-618-64113-0

9 1421 11

4500331386

4-1

Name ______________________________

Homework

Use the picture graph to answer the questions.

Book Sales

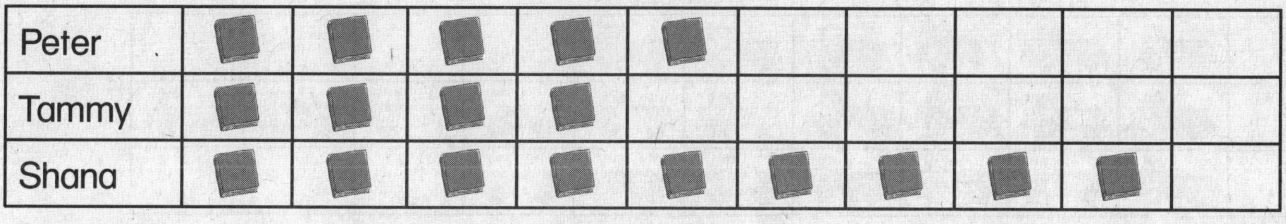

1. Who sold the most books? ____________________

2. Who sold the fewest books? ____________________

3. How many more books did Shana sell than Tammy?

☐ ____________________
label

4. How many fewer books did Peter sell than Shana?

☐ ____________________
label

5. How many more books did Peter sell than Tammy?

☐ ____________________
label

6. How many books did the children sell altogether?

☐ ____________________
label

7. Write Your Own Write and solve your own question about the graph.

____

____

4-1 Name ______________________

Targeted Practice

Use the picture graph to answer the questions.

Trucks Made in the Toy Shop

1. Who made the most trucks? ______________

2. Who made the fewest trucks? ______________

3. How many more trucks did Leroy make than Misha?

☐ ______________
label

4. How many fewer trucks did Ella make than Leroy?

☐ ______________
label

5. How many more trucks did Ella make than Misha?

☐ ______________
label

6. How many trucks did the children make altogether?

☐ ______________
label

7. Write Your Own Write and solve your own question about the graph.

____

____

4-2 **Name** ____________________

Homework

Compare to find how many **more** or **fewer**.
Write the number. Ring *more* or *fewer*.

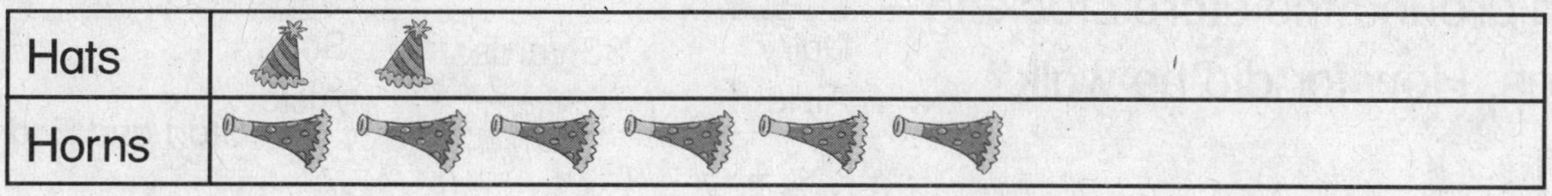

1. There are ☐ *more fewer* hats than horns.

2. There are ☐ *more fewer* horns than hats.

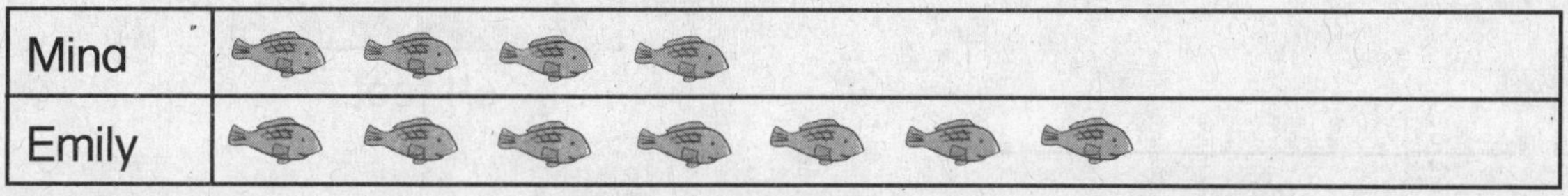

3. Mina has ☐ *more fewer* goldfish than Emily.

4. Emily has ☐ *more fewer* goldfish than Mina.

5. Dan has ☐ *more fewer* bells than Tani.

6. Tani has ☐ *more fewer* bells than Dan.

Name ______________________________

Remembering

Solve each story problem.

1. Here is the path Mr. Green took as he walked around the store stocking the shelves. How far did he walk?

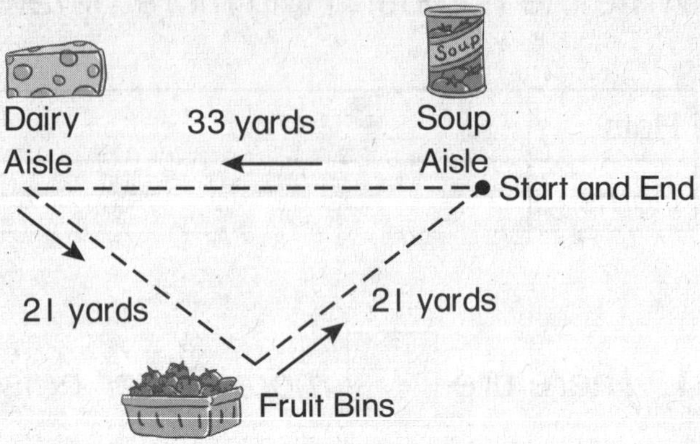

☐ ______________________
label

2. Rose is helping to put a fence around her family's backyard. How much fencing should they buy?

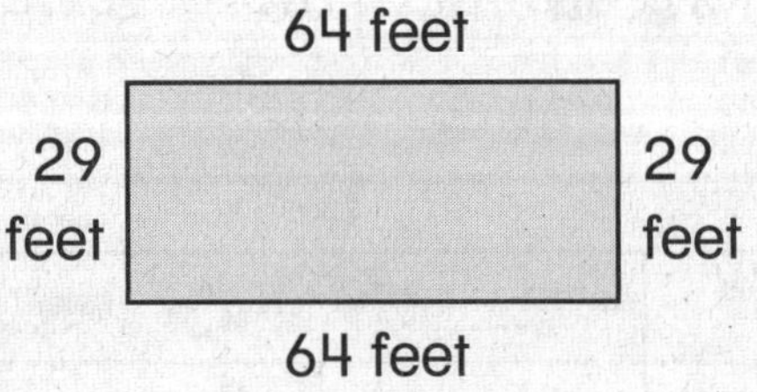

☐ ______________________
label

Add ones or tens. Make a Proof Drawing if it helps you.

3. 9 + 8 = ______

90 + 80 = ______

4. 7 + 7 = ______

70 + 70 = ______

5. 8 + 7 = ______

80 + 70 = ______

6. 6 + 5 = ______

60 + 50 = ______

7. Find the unknown partner.

100

29 ☐

4-3

Name ____________________

Homework

Compare. Ring the extra amount.
Write the number. Then ring *more* or *fewer.*

Pumpkins

Martin	
Kerra	

1. Martin has ☐ *more fewer* pumpkins than Kerra.

2. Kerra has ☐ *more fewer* pumpkins than Martin.

3. Martin needs ☐ pumpkins to have as many as Kerra.

4. Kerra must lose ☐ pumpkins to have as many as Martin.

Compare these numbers. Write the **is greater than** (>) or **is less than** (<) sign in the circle. The first one is done for you.

5. 5 (<) 8 9 ◯ 3 6 ◯ 7

6. 1 ◯ 4 8 ◯ 6 4 ◯ 3

7. 6 ◯ 5 3 ◯ 7 9 ◯ 8

8. 5 ◯ 2 7 ◯ 9 1 ◯ 2

Name ______________________

Targeted Practice

Compare. Ring the extra amount.
Write the number. Then ring *more* or *fewer*.

Peppers

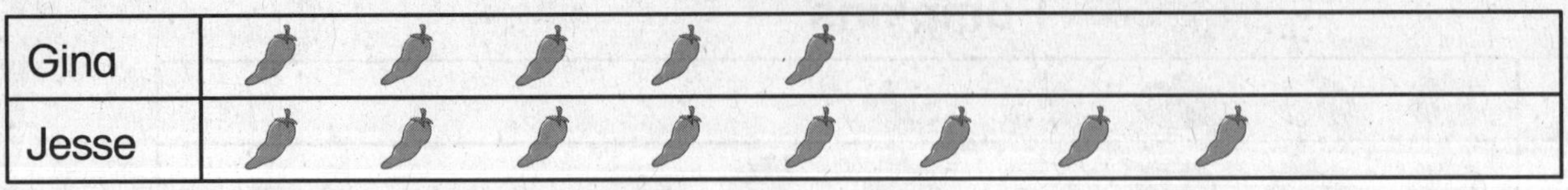

1. Gina has ☐ *more fewer* peppers than Jesse.

2. Jesse has ☐ *more fewer* peppers than Gina.

3. Gina needs ☐ peppers to have as many as Jesse.

4. Jesse must give away ☐ peppers to have as many as Gina.

Bears

5. Marco has ☐ *more fewer* bears than Alena.

6. Alena has ☐ *more fewer* bears than Marco.

7. Marco needs ☐ bears to have as many as Alena.

8. Alena must give away ☐ bears to have as many as Marco.

Name ____________________

Homework

Solve each story problem.	Show your work.
1. Yesterday, Annie saw 17 ducks at the park. Cristina saw 8 ducks. How many more ducks did Annie see than Cristina? ☐ ____________ label	
2. Juan made 6 fruit cups for the picnic this afternoon. Teresa made 9 more fruit cups than Juan. How many fruit cups did Teresa make? ☐ ____________ label	
3. Michelle collected 13 baseballs. Rini collected 7 baseballs. How many more baseballs does Rini have to collect to have as many baseballs as Michelle? ☐ ____________ label	
4. Tom has 12 horses on his farm. He has 4 fewer chickens than horses. How many chickens does Tom have? ☐ ____________ label	

Name ____________________

Remembering

Solve each story problem.

Show your work.

1. Mr. Gomez has 75 cans of beans. Each shelf holds 10 cans. How many shelves can he fill with cans of beans? How many cans will be left over?

☐ shelves ☐ cans left over

2. Abigail has 39 stamps in her collection. She puts 10 stamps on each page of her stamp book. How many pages can she fill with stamps? How many stamps will be left over?

☐ pages ☐ stamps left over

Add.

3. 45 + 8 = ____ 22 + 4 = ____ 86 + 3 = ____

Add.

4. 60 + 20 = ____ 90 + 80 = ____ 70 + 30 = ____

6 + 2 = ____ 9 + 8 = ____ 7 + 3 = ____

5. 50 + 70 = ____ 40 + 90 = ____ 20 + 40 = ____

5 + 7 = ____ 4 + 9 = ____ 2 + 4 = ____

6. Find the unknown partner.

100

☐ 54

4-5

Name

Homework

Use the table. Fill in the boxes with numbers.
Ring *more* or *fewer*.

	Toys	Games
Jake	5	9
Kara	8	4

1. Jake has ☐ *more fewer* games than Kara.

2. Kara has ☐ *more fewer* games than Jake.

3. Kara has ☐ *more fewer* toys than Jake.

4. Jake has ☐ *more fewer* toys than Kara.

5. The children have ☐ games altogether.

6. The children have ☐ toys altogether.

7. Kara must give away ☐ toys to have as many as Jake.

8. Kara must get ☐ games to have as many as Jake.

Name ____________________

Targeted Practice

Use the table. Fill in the boxes with numbers.
Ring *more* or *fewer*.

	Books	CDs
Meg	7	2
Kate	9	5
Andrew	3	8

1. Kate has ☐ *more fewer* CDs than Andrew.

2. Meg has ☐ *more fewer* books than Kate.

3. Andrew has ☐ *more fewer* CDs than Kate.

4. The children have ☐ books altogether.

5. Meg needs ☐ books to have as many as Kate.

6. Andrew must get ☐ books to have as many as Meg.

7. Meg must get ☐ CDs to have as many as Andrew.

8. Kate and Andrew have a total of ☐ CDs.

Name ____________________

Homework

Chen has 7 markers. Linda has 4 markers.

1. Make a table to show this.

____

2. Turn the table into a picture graph.

Use a circle for each  .

____

Compare. Circle the extra amount in the graph above.
Write the number. Then ring *more* or *fewer* below.

3. Linda has ☐ *more* *fewer* markers than Chen.

4. Chen has ☐ *more* *fewer* markers than Linda.

5. Linda needs ☐ markers to have as many as Chen.

6. Chen must lose ☐ markers to have as many as Linda.

 Name ______________________________

Remembering

Solve the story problem.	Show your work.
1. Mrs. Green put away 63 bags of peanuts. Mr. Green put away 58 bags of peanuts. How many bags of peanuts did they put away in all? ☐ ______________ label	

Compare. Ring the extra amount.
Write the number. Then ring *more* or *fewer*.

Mr. Green	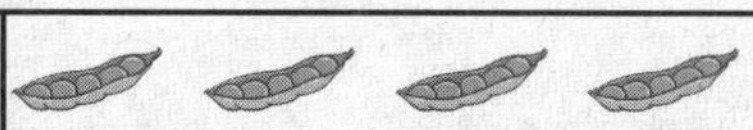
Mrs. Green	

2. Mr. Green has ☐ *more* *fewer* peapods than Mrs. Green.

3. Mr. Green needs ☐ peapods to have as many as Mrs. Green.

Compare. Write the **is greater than** (>) or **is less than** (<) sign in the circle.

4. 3 ◯ 9 8 ◯ 6 4 ◯ 2

5. 7 ◯ 1 2 ◯ 4 6 ◯ 5

6. Find the unknown partner.

100

☐ 47

Name ______________________________

Homework

1. Prince won 8 medals at the dog show. Lady won 5 medals. Muffy won 3 medals. Make a table to show this.

____

2. Turn the table into a picture graph. Use a circle for each .

____

Compare. Write the number. Ring *more* or *fewer*.

3. Prince has ☐ *more fewer* medals than Muffy.

4. Muffy has ☐ *more fewer* medals than Prince.

5. Lady needs ☐ medals to have as many as Prince.

6. Lady must lose ☐ medals to have as many as Muffy.

Name ______________________________

Targeted Practice

Beth and Hamal like to go hiking and biking.
The table shows how many miles the children traveled.

Number of Miles Traveled

	Hiking	Biking	Total
Beth	19	47	
Hamal	36	48	
Total			

1. How many miles did Hamal travel in all? ______ miles
Put this in the table.

2. How many miles did Beth travel in all? ______ miles
Put this in the table.

3. How many miles did the children hike? ______ miles
Put this in the table.

4. How many miles did the children bike? ______ miles
Put this in the table.

5. How many miles did the children travel altogether? ______ miles
Put this in the table.

6. Find the total number of miles the children hiked. ______ miles
The partners are ______ and ______.

7. Find the total number of miles the children biked. ______ miles
The partners are ______ and ______.

8. Find the total number of miles Beth traveled. ______ miles
The partners are ______ and ______.

9. Find the total number of miles Hamal traveled. ______ miles
The partners are ______ and ______.

Name ____________________

Homework

1. The park has 9 oak trees, 2 maple trees, and 6 elm trees in it. Complete the table to show this.

Trees in the Park

Oak	
Maple	
Elm	

2. Use the data table to complete the bar graph.

Trees in the Park

Oak										
Maple										
Elm										
	0	1	2	3	4	5	6	7	8	9	10

Use your bar graph. Fill in the missing number and ring *more* or *fewer*.

3. There are ☐ *more* *fewer* oak trees than maple trees in the park.

4. There are ☐ *more* *fewer* maple trees than elm trees in the park.

5. We need to plant ☐ *more* *fewer* elm trees to have as many elm trees as oak trees.

Name

Remembering

1. Write the total amount of money.

______

Use the table to answer the questions. Fill in the boxes with the numbers. Ring *more* or *fewer* if you need to.

	Nickels	Dimes
Jessica	7	3
Eddie	4	5

2. Jessica has ☐ *more* *fewer* nickels than Eddie.

3. Eddie has ☐ *more* *fewer* nickels than Jessica.

4. Eddie must give away ☐ dimes to have as many dimes as Jessica.

Add.

5. 100 + 96 = ____ 62 + 100 = ____ 100 + 7 = ____

10 + 96 = ____ 62 + 10 = ____ 10 + 7 = ____

1 + 96 = ____ 62 + 1 = ____ 1 + 7 = ____

4-9

Homework

Name ______________________

Use the bar graph to complete the sentences.
Ring *more* or *fewer*.

Instruments My Friends Play

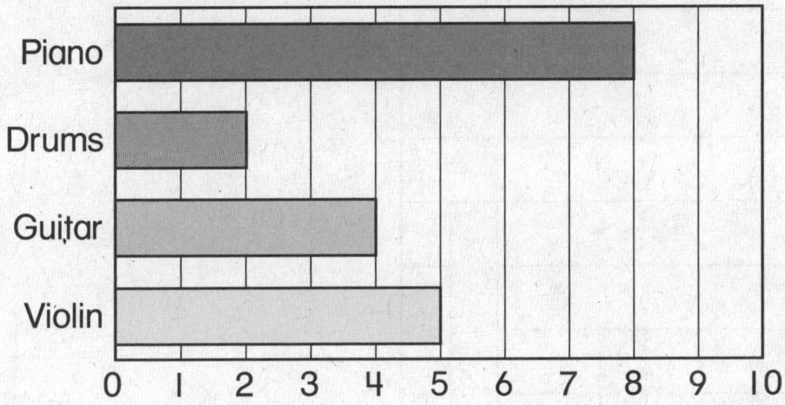

1. ☐ *more fewer* children play the drums than the guitar.

2. ☐ *more fewer* children play the drums than the violin.

3. ☐ *more fewer* children play the piano than the drums.

4. ☐ *more fewer* children play the piano than the guitar.

5. ☐ *more fewer* children play the violin than the piano.

6. ☐ children play the piano or the drums.

7. ☐ children play the piano, guitar, and violin altogether.

 Name

Targeted Practice

Use the bar graph to complete the sentences.
Ring *more* or *fewer*.

School Supplies on the Shelf

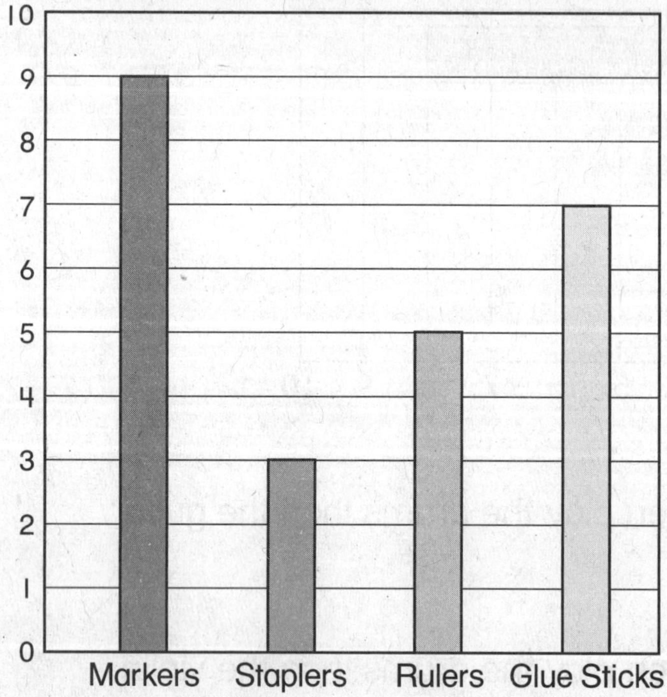

1. There are ☐ *more* *fewer* markers on the shelf than rulers.
2. There are ☐ *more* *fewer* staplers on the shelf than glue sticks.
3. There are ☐ *more* *fewer* markers on the shelf than staplers.
4. There are ☐ *more* *fewer* glue sticks on the shelf than rulers.
5. There are ☐ *more* *fewer* rulers on the shelf than staplers.
6. There are *more* *fewer* markers than there are rulers and staplers combined.
7. There is a total of ☐ glue sticks and markers.

4-10 Name ______

Homework

Use the bar graph to answer the questions below.
Fill in the circle next to the correct answer.

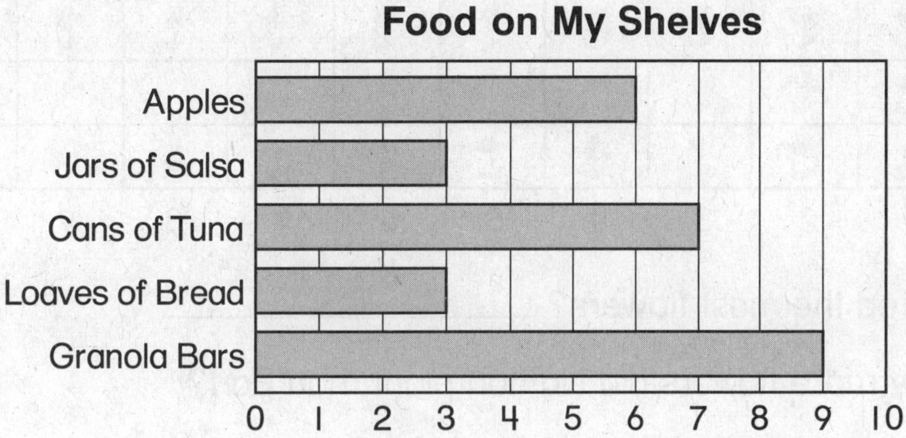

1. How many more cans of tuna are there than jars of salsa?

○ 4
○ 5
○ 6
○ 7

2. Altogether, how many apples and granola bars do I have?

○ 11
○ 13
○ 15
○ 16

3. I have the same number of which two foods?

○ Apples and granola bars
○ Apples and tuna
○ Salsa and bread
○ Tuna and granola bars

4. Write Your Own Write 1 question about the graph. Answer your question.

______

______

 Name ______________________________

Remembering

Use the picture graph to answer the questions.

Flowers Planted in the Garden

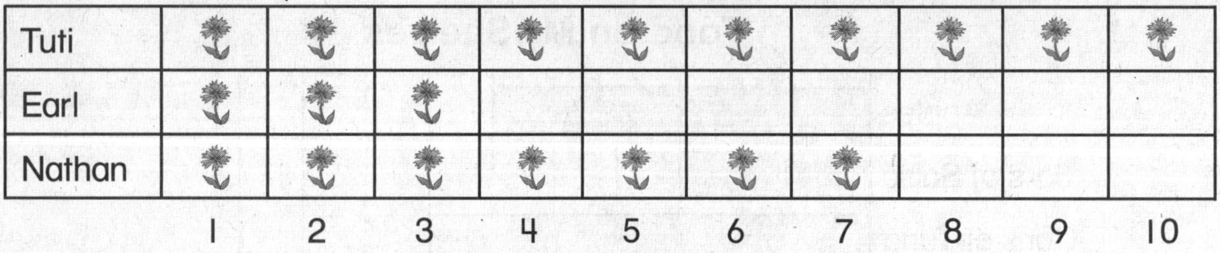

1. Who planted the most flowers? ______________

2. How many more flowers did Nathan plant than Earl?

☐ ______________
label

3. How many fewer flowers did Earl plant than Tuti?

☐ ______________
label

Add. Make a Proof Drawing if it helps.

4. $\begin{array}{r} 76 \\ +\ 39 \\ \hline \end{array}$ $\begin{array}{r} 43 \\ +\ 78 \\ \hline \end{array}$ $\begin{array}{r} 52 \\ +\ 87 \\ \hline \end{array}$

5. $\begin{array}{r} 61 \\ +\ 75 \\ \hline \end{array}$ $\begin{array}{r} 57 \\ +\ 98 \\ \hline \end{array}$ $\begin{array}{r} 89 \\ +\ 48 \\ \hline \end{array}$

6. Find the unknown partner.

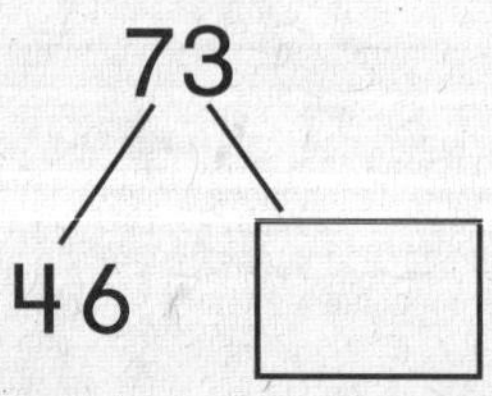

Name ______________________________

Homework

Use the information in the circle graph to answer the questions below. Fill in the circle next to the correct answer.

Toys in the Playroom

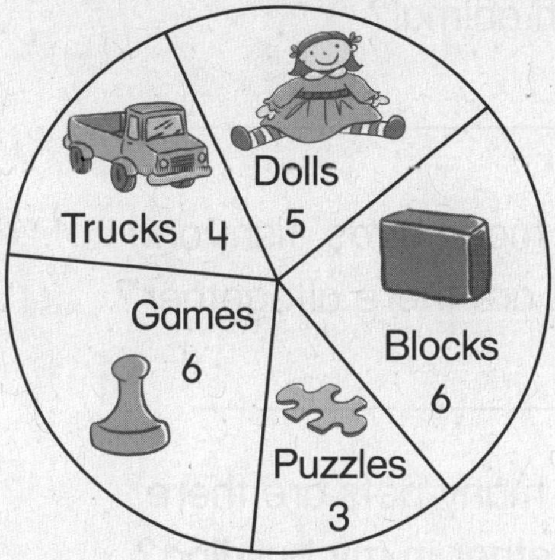

1. The teacher told Brandie to bring her all of the dolls and games. How many toys does Brandie have to bring to the teacher?

- ○ 9
- ○ 10
- ○ 11
- ○ 12

2. How many more blocks are there than trucks?

- ○ 1
- ○ 2
- ○ 4
- ○ 6

3. The playroom has the same number of which two kinds of toys?

- ○ blocks and dolls
- ○ dolls and puzzles
- ○ games and blocks
- ○ trucks and puzzles

4. There is 1 fewer truck than __________.

- ○ blocks
- ○ dolls
- ○ games
- ○ puzzles

5. There are 3 more games than __________.

- ○ blocks
- ○ dolls
- ○ puzzles
- ○ trucks

Name ______________________________

Targeted Practice

Use the information in the circle graph to answer the questions.

Pets in My Building

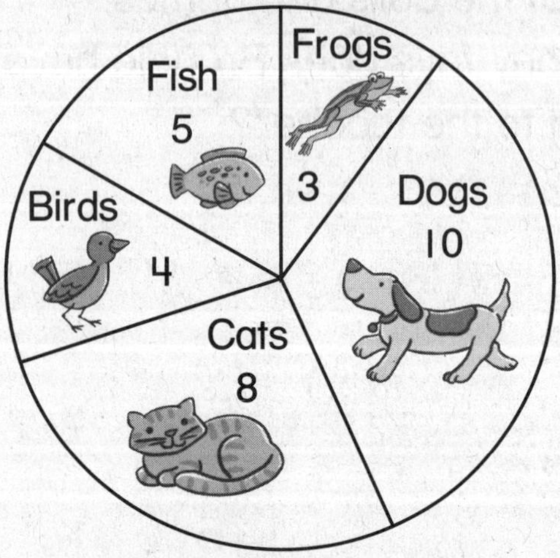

1. My building has the most of which animal?

____

2. How many birds, fish, and frogs are there altogether?

____

3. How many pets are there altogether in my building?

____

4. How many more dogs are there than frogs?

____

5. How many fewer fish are there than cats?

____

Use the information in the circle graph to complete each sentence.

6. There is 1 fewer bird than there are ______________________.

7. There are 3 more cats than there are ______________________.

8. There is 1 more bird than there are ______________________.

9. There are 2 fewer cats than there are ______________________.

Name ______________________

Homework

Use the information in the circle graph to answer the questions below. Fill in the circle next to the correct answer.

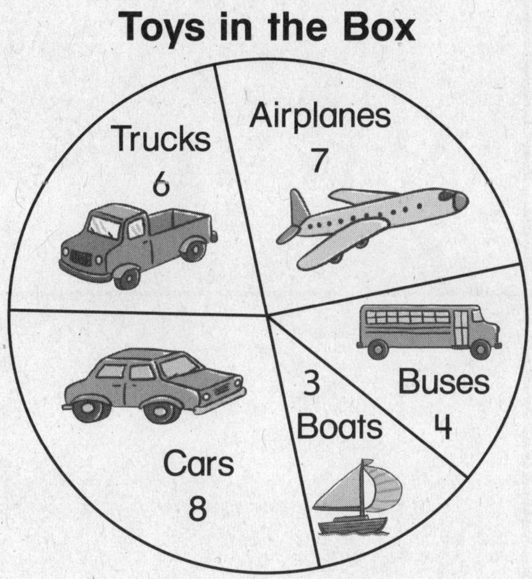

1. There is 1 fewer truck than there are ________.

- ◯ airplanes
- ◯ boats
- ◯ buses
- ◯ cars

2. There are 2 more trucks than there are ________.

- ◯ airplanes
- ◯ boats
- ◯ buses
- ◯ cars

3. There are 5 fewer boats than there are ________.

- ◯ airplanes
- ◯ boats
- ◯ cars
- ◯ trucks

4. How many cars, boats, and airplanes are there in the box?

- ◯ 17
- ◯ 18
- ◯ 20
- ◯ 28

5. What is the total number of buses and trucks in the box?

- ◯ 4
- ◯ 8
- ◯ 10
- ◯ 12

Name ______________________

Remembering

Solve the story problems. | **Show your work.**

1. Erin has 14 shirts in her closet. Vana has 6 shirts in her closet. How many more shirts does Erin have than Vana?

☐ ______________________
label

2. 17 people went to Hoon's party. 9 people went to Mark's party. How many fewer people were at Mark's party than Hoon's?

☐ ______________________
label

Is the answer correct?
Write *yes* or *no*. If *no*, fix the exercise.

3. $37 + 65 = 102$ OK? ☐

4. $57 + 26 = 73$ OK? ☐

5. $42 + 59 = 911$ OK? ☐

6. $17 + 45 = 71$ OK? ☐

7. $69 + 13 = 72$ OK? ☐

8. $51 + 35 = 86$ OK? ☐

9. Find the unknown partner.

100
☐ 88

Name ______________________________

Homework

1. Complete the horizontal bar graph using the information given below.

- Jun has 5 marbles.
- Angela has 3 more marbles than Jun.
- Janell has to lose 4 marbles to have as many as Jun.
- Caroline has 2 fewer marbles than Angela.

Marbles We Have

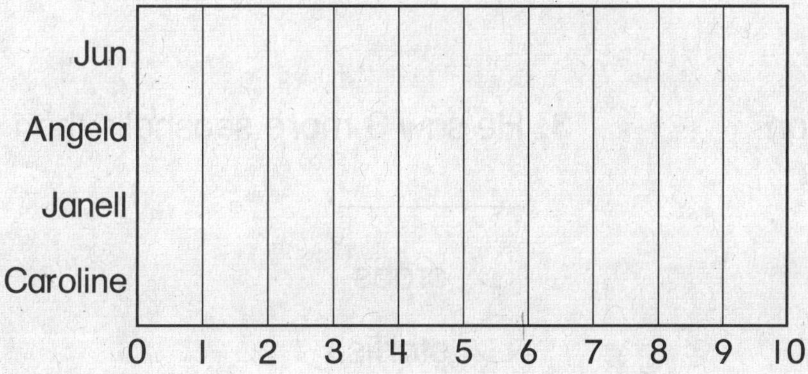

Compare the numbers below. Use **is greater than** (>) or **is less than** (<). The first one is done for you.

2. 6 (<) 9   7 ◯ 4   2 ◯ 3

3. 8 ◯ 5   1 ◯ 10   4 ◯ 1

4. 6 ◯ 0   8 ◯ 3   7 ◯ 8

 Name ____________________

Remembering

Use the information in the circle graph to answer the questions below. Fill in the circle next to the correct answer.

What Jared Saw at the Beach

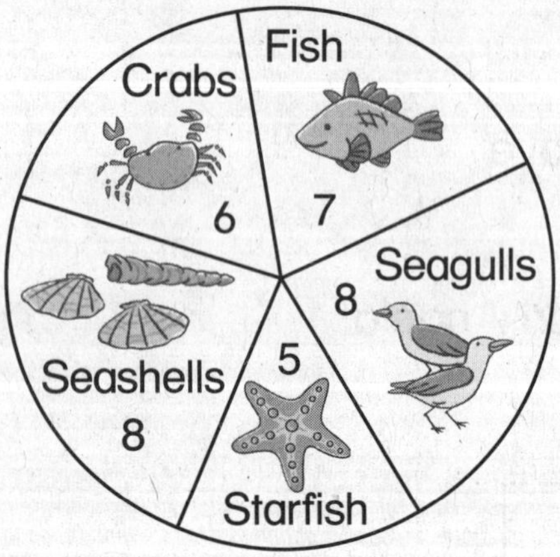

1. How many more seagulls did Jared see than fish?

- ○ 1
- ○ 2
- ○ 4
- ○ 5

2. He saw 1 fewer crab than ________.

- ○ starfish
- ○ fish
- ○ seagull
- ○ seashell

3. He saw 3 more seashells than ________.

- ○ crabs
- ○ starfish
- ○ fish
- ○ seagulls

Complete the number sequence. Write the rule.

4. 12, 20, 28, ________, ________, ________ Rule: *n* ________

5. 38, 41, 44, ________, ________, ________ Rule: *n* ________

6. 93, 88, 83, ________, ________, ________ Rule: *n* ________

---

7. Find the unknown partner.

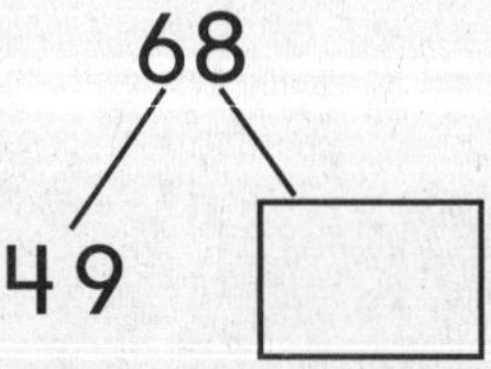

Name ______________________________

Homework

Lena and Paulo test light bulbs. The table shows what they found. Answer each question and fill in the table with your answers.

Working Light Bulbs

	Green	Yellow	Total
Paulo	47	51	
Lena	38	29	
Total			

1. How many green bulbs worked? ______ green bulbs

2. How many of Paulo's bulbs worked? ______ bulbs

3. How many of Lena's bulbs worked? ______ bulbs

4. How many bulbs worked in total? ______ bulbs

Use the bar graph to answer the questions.

Bike Trails (in miles)

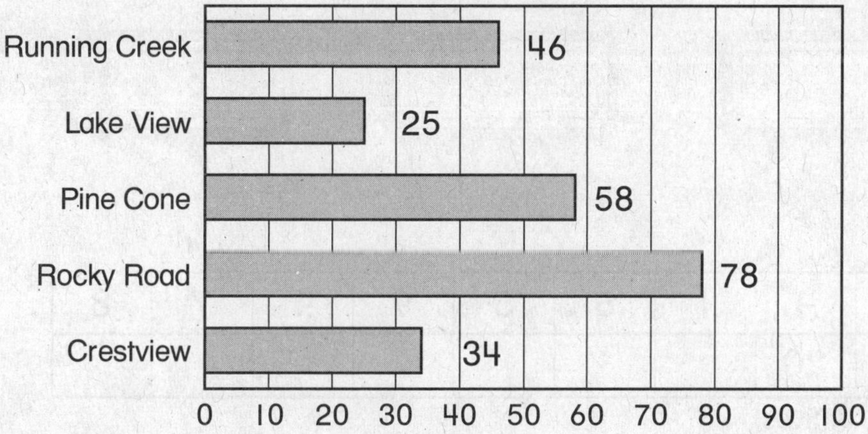

5. A bike race is held on Pine Cone and Lake View trails. How long is the race?

__________ miles

6. You want to ride exactly 80 miles this week. Which two trails should you take?

______________ and

____

7. How far will you go if you ride Pine Cone and Rocky Road?

__________ miles

Name ____________________

Remembering

Draw the hands on the clock to show the time.

1.

Write the time on the digital clock.

2.

Complete the tables.

3.

Big hand points to	4	1	6	5	9	4	7	8
Time in minutes	20							

(4 fives)

4.

Big hand points to	8	11	10	6	9	7	5	3
Time in minutes	40							

(8 fives)

5. Find the unknown partner.

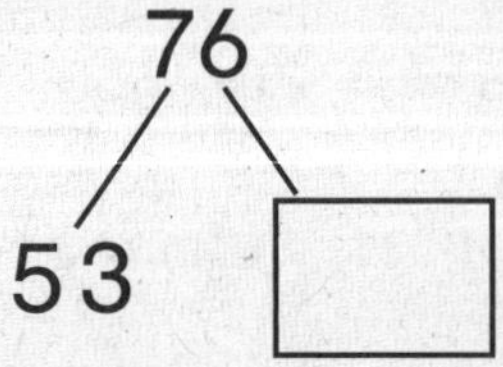

D–1

Name ______________________

Homework

	Draw one diagonal.	Draw the other diagonal.	Draw both diagonals.
1.			
2.	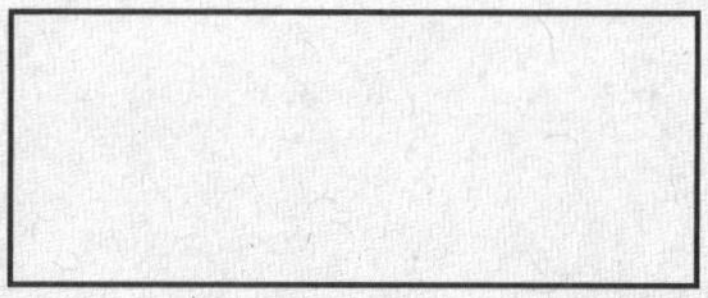	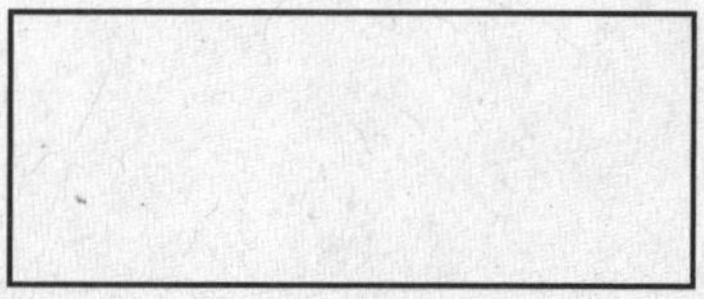	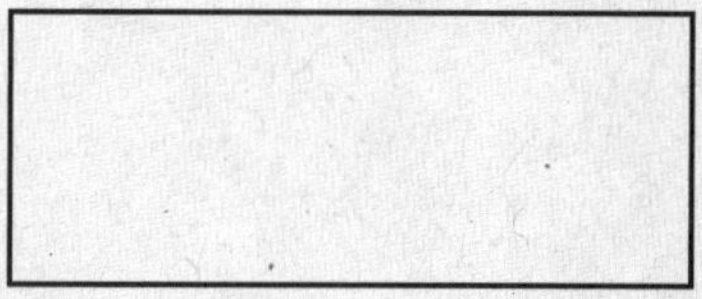
3.	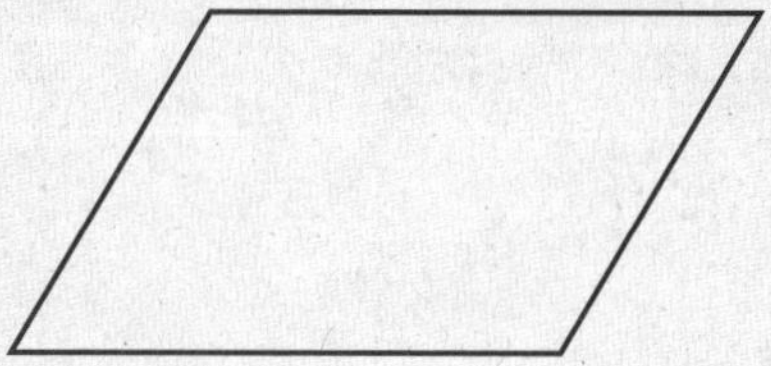	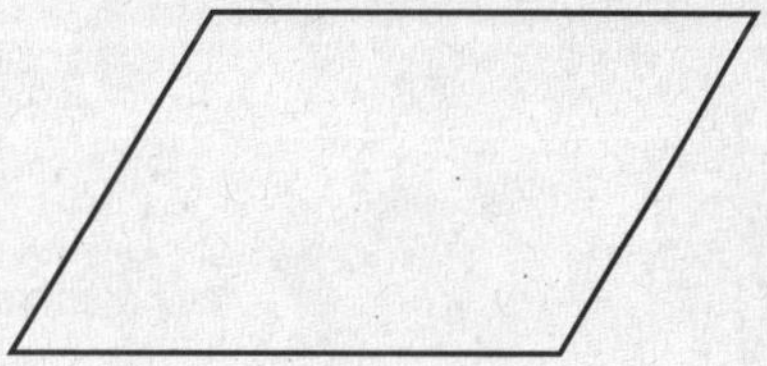	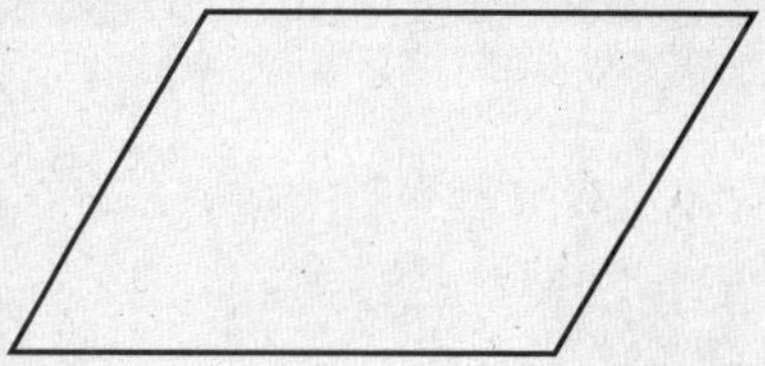
4.	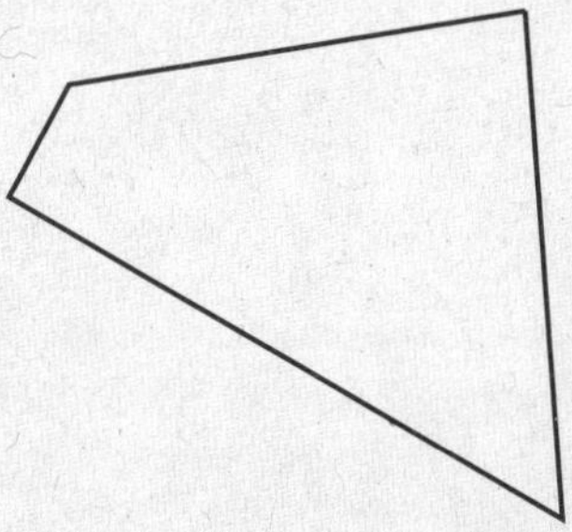	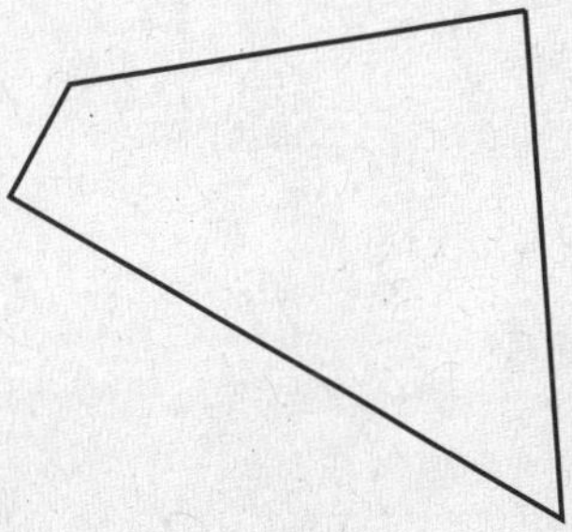	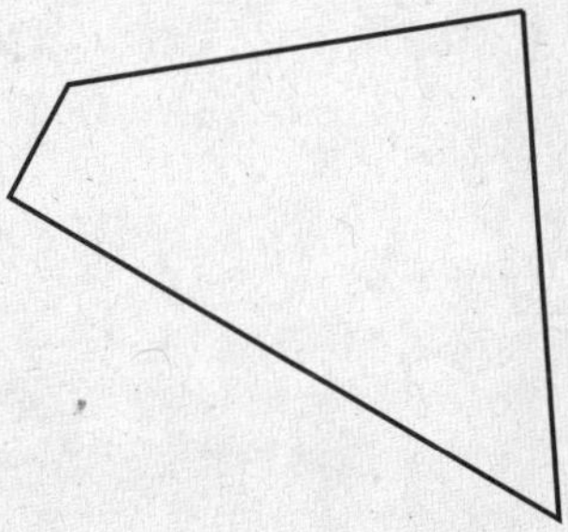

5. **On the Back** Find an object in your home that is a quadrilateral and use a ruler to draw a picture of it. Draw two diagonals. What shapes did you form by drawing the two diagonals?

Name

D–2

Name ____________________

Homework

Use estimation to find the midpoints.

	Connect the midpoints of two opposite sides.	Connect the midpoints of the other two sides.	Draw both line segments.
1.			
2.			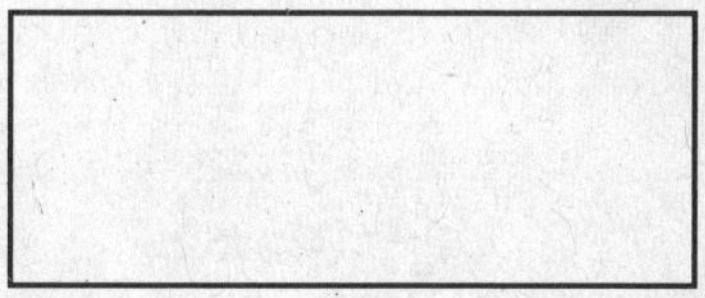
3.	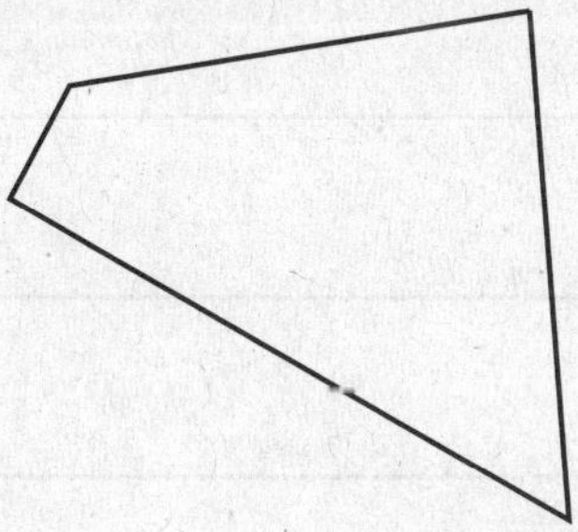	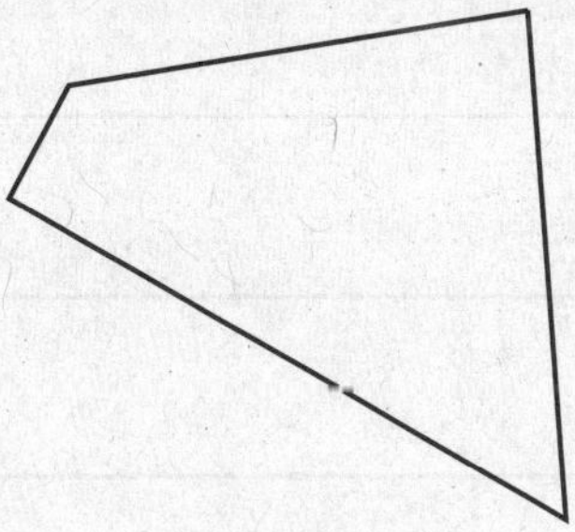	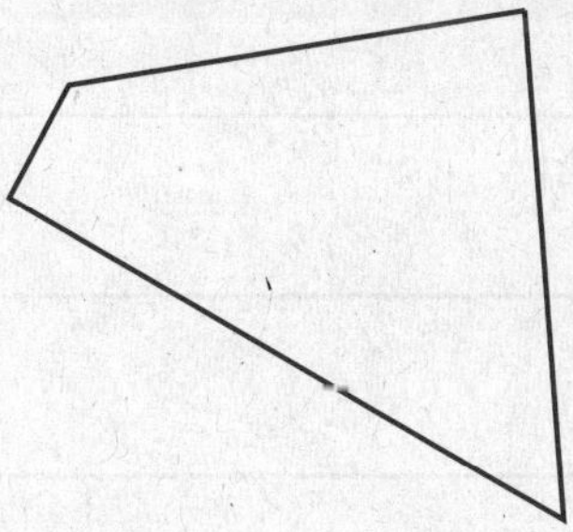

4. On the Back Find an object in the shape of a quadrilateral in your home.

- Use a centimeter ruler to draw the object.
- Estimate the position of the midpoint on each side.
- Connect the midpoints of opposite sides.
- Describe the shapes that you see.

Name

D–3

Name ______________________________

Homework

	Draw one diagonal.	Draw the other diagonal.	Draw both diagonals.
1.			
2.	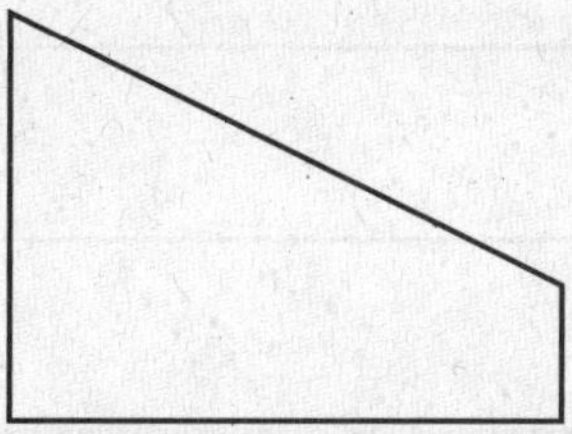	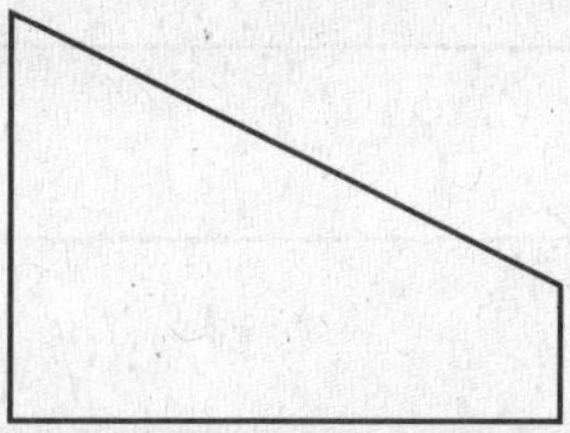	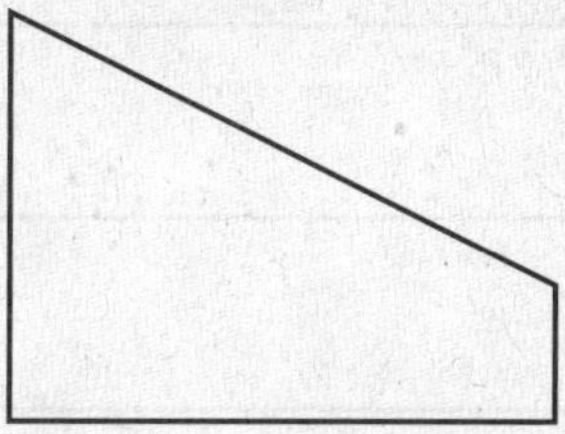

	Connect the midpoints of two opposite sides.	Connect the midpoints of the other two sides.	Draw both line segments.
3.			
4.	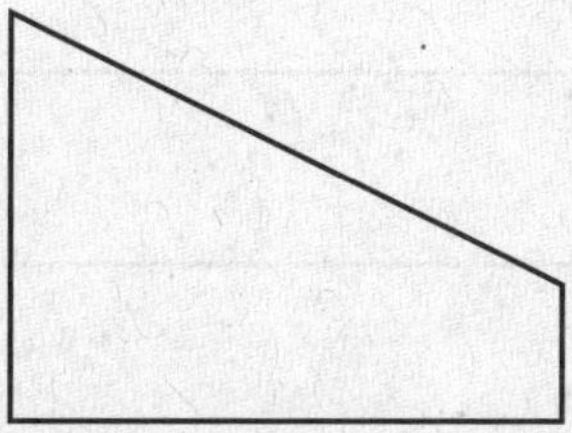	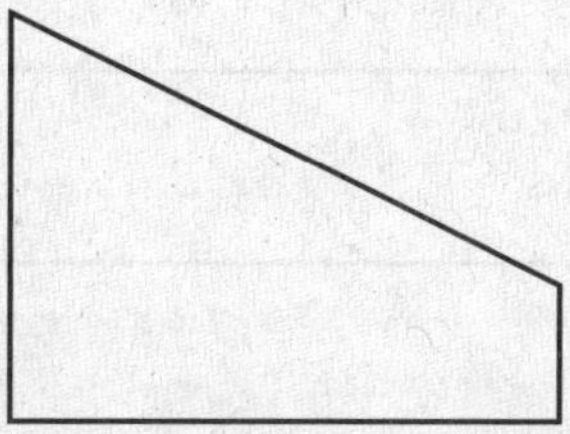	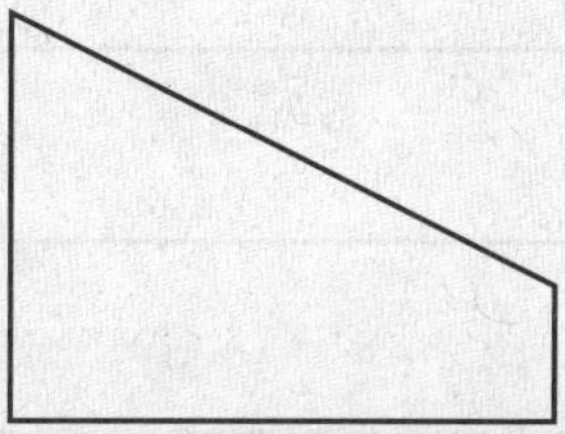

5. On the Back For each shape above, tell about the new shapes you made.

Name

5–1

Homework

Name ______________________

Draw coins to show 6 different ways to make 25¢ with pennies, nickels, and/or dimes.

1. 25¢	2. 25¢	3. 25¢
4. 25¢	5. 25¢	6. 25¢

Write how to count the money.

7. 

25¢ 50¢ ____ ____ ____ ____ ____ ____ ____

8. 

25¢ 50¢ ____ ____ ____ ____ ____

Name ____________________

Targeted Practice

Use the bar graph to answer the questions below. Write your answers in the boxes. Ring *more* or *fewer*.

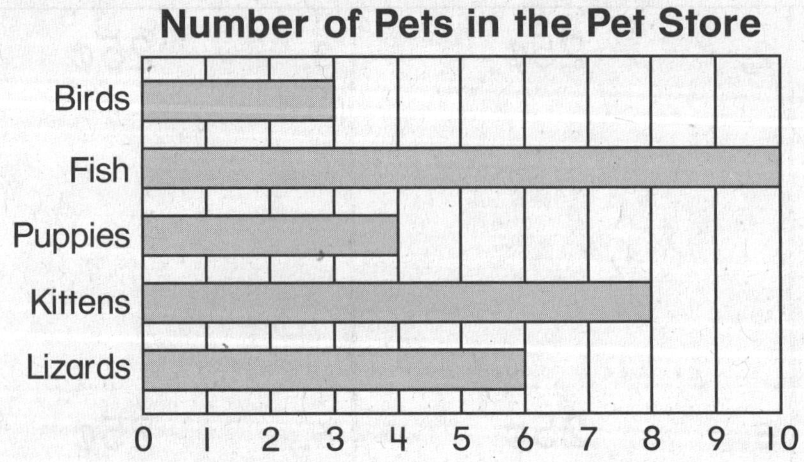

1. There are ☐ *more* *fewer* birds in the pet store than lizards.

2. There are ☐ *more* *fewer* puppies in the pet store than kittens.

3. There are ☐ *more* *fewer* fish in the pet store than birds.

4. There are ☐ *more* *fewer* lizards in the pet store than kittens.

5. There are ☐ *more* *fewer* puppies in the pet store than fish.

6. There are *more* *fewer* fish than there are birds and lizards combined.

7. There is a total of ☐ puppies and kittens.

5–2

Name ______________________

Homework

Draw coins to show 6 different ways to make $1.00.
Use pennies, nickels, dimes, and/or quarters.

1. $1.00	2. $1.00
3. $1.00	4. $1.00
5. $1.00	6. $1.00

Name ______

Remembering

Complete the number sequence. Write the rule.

1. 75, 69, 63, ______, ______, ______ Rule: n ______

2. 34, 41, 48, ______, ______, ______ Rule: n ______

Add.

3. 100 + 71 = ______ 6 + 100 = ______

10 + 71 = ______ 6 + 10 = ______

1 + 71 = ______ 6 + 1 = ______

Add.

4. $\begin{array}{r} 73 \\ +\ 30 \\ \hline \end{array}$

5. $\begin{array}{r} 64 \\ +\ 99 \\ \hline \end{array}$

6. $\begin{array}{r} 26 \\ +\ 58 \\ \hline \end{array}$

Solve the story problem.	Show your work.
7. Mr. Green worked at the store 57 hours last week. Mrs. Green worked the same number of hours. How many hours did they work in total? ☐ ______ label	

8. **Geometry** Draw a diagonal.

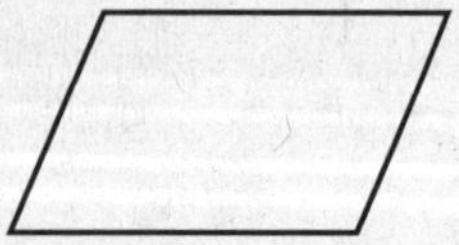

5–3 **Name** ______________________

Homework

Solve the story problems. Rewrite the 100 or make a drawing. Add to check your answer.

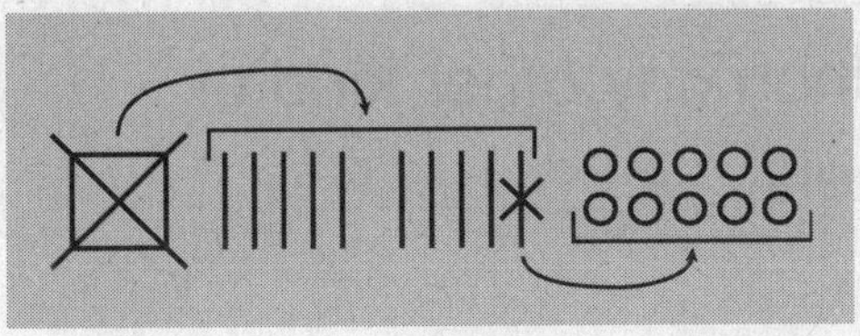

$$\begin{array}{rl} & \quad\ \ ^{90}\quad ^{10} \\ 100 = & \not{1}\not{0}\not{0} + \not{0} \\ -\ 68 = & 60 + 8 \\ \hline & 30 + 2 = 32 \end{array}$$

Tens	Ones
9	10

$$\begin{array}{r} \not{1}\not{0}\not{0} \\ -\ 68 \\ \hline 32 \end{array}$$

---

1. There were 100 rubber ducks in the river race. 19 of them sank. How many ducks are in the race now?

☐ ______________________
label

---

2. Ben bought 100 napkins for the picnic. We used 74 of them. How many napkins were left?

☐ ______________________
label

Find the unknown partner. Check by adding.

3.

100	100	100	100
85 ☐	67 ☐	58 ☐	23 ☐

Name ______________________________

Targeted Practice

Use the information in the circle graph to answer the questions below. Fill in the blanks.

Weather This Month (Number of Days)

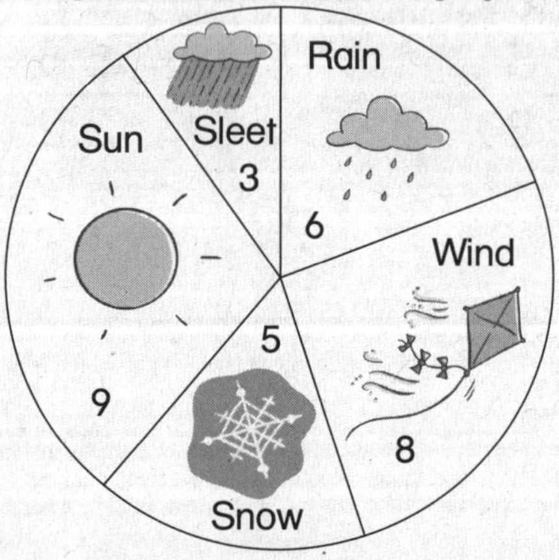

1. We had ____________ on more days than any other kind of weather.

2. We had rain 1 more day than we had ____________.

3. We had snow 4 fewer days than we had ____________.

4. We had wind 5 more days than we had ____________.

5. We had sun and snow for the same total number of days as we had ____________ and ____________.

Write two other things the circle graph shows.

____

____

____

____

____

____

____

____

Name ______________________

Homework

Solve the story problems. Make a Proof Drawing if you need to.	Show your work.
1. Amon had 94 tomato seeds. He used 27 of them for a science project. How many seeds did he have left? ☐ ______ label	
2. Benita made 56 leaf prints. She gave 29 prints to her cousins. How many prints does Benita have now? ☐ ______ label	
3. Denise had 71 straws. She used 33 of them to make a bridge. How many straws does she have left? ☐ ______ label	
4. Cedric had 70 sports cards. He gave away 24 cards to his friends. How many cards does Cedric have now? ☐ ______ label	

Name ____________________

Remembering

Add.

1. $45 + 93$

2. $72 + 59$

3. $48 + 23$

4. Draw coins to show two ways to make 25¢.

25¢	25¢

Solve the story problem. **Show your work.**

5. Josh solved 8 math problems. If he had solved another 7 problems he would have solved as many as Mato. How many problems did Mato solve?

☐ ____________________
label

6. Geometry

Connect midpoints of two opposite sides.	Connect midpoints of the other two opposite sides.	Draw both line segments.
▭	▭	▭

5–5 Name

Homework

The Expanded Method

$$\begin{array}{rcl} 93 & = & \overset{80}{\cancel{90}} + \overset{13}{\cancel{3}} \\ -\,57 & = & 50 + 7 \\ \hline & & 30 + 6 = 36 \end{array}$$

The Ungrouping First Method

$$\begin{array}{r} \overset{8\ \ 13}{\cancel{9}\cancel{3}} \\ -\,57 \\ \hline 36 \end{array}$$

Proof Drawing

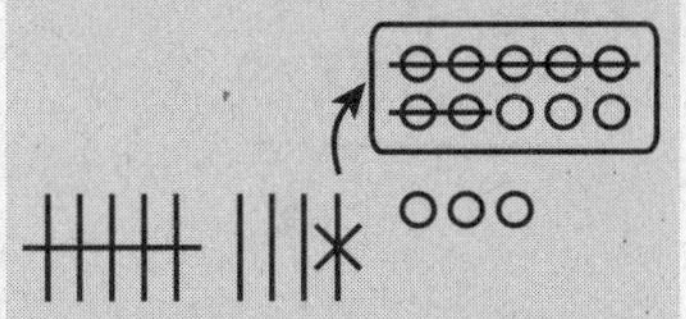

Subtract using any method.

1. 38 − 21 = ____

2. 57 − 39 = ____

3. 95 − 64 = ____

4. 50 − 13 = ____

5. 68 − 15 = ____

6. 77 − 29 = ____

7. 74 − 48 = ____

8. 84 − 49 = ____

Name ____________________

Targeted Practice

Subtract.

1. 64 − 37

2. 81 − 34

3. 48 − 26

4. 73 − 19

5. 96 − 58

6. 55 − 26

7. 67 − 52

8. 71 − 45

9. 43 − 15

10. 38 − 14

11. 50 − 31

12. 94 − 57

13. 76 − 38

14. 85 − 67

15. 84 − 49

Name ____________________

Homework

Subtract.

1. $\begin{array}{r} 87 \\ -\ 59 \\ \hline \end{array}$

2. $\begin{array}{r} 63 \\ -\ 14 \\ \hline \end{array}$

3. $\begin{array}{r} 55 \\ -\ 18 \\ \hline \end{array}$

4. $\begin{array}{r} 73 \\ -\ 17 \\ \hline \end{array}$

5. $\begin{array}{r} 83 \\ -\ 12 \\ \hline \end{array}$

6. $\begin{array}{r} 99 \\ -\ 35 \\ \hline \end{array}$

7. $\begin{array}{r} 62 \\ -\ 55 \\ \hline \end{array}$

8. $\begin{array}{r} 71 \\ -\ 49 \\ \hline \end{array}$

9. $\begin{array}{r} 45 \\ -\ 26 \\ \hline \end{array}$

10. $\begin{array}{r} 50 \\ -\ 11 \\ \hline \end{array}$

11. $\begin{array}{r} 92 \\ -\ 44 \\ \hline \end{array}$

12. $\begin{array}{r} 75 \\ -\ 52 \\ \hline \end{array}$

Name ______________________________

Remembering

Answer the questions below by reading the circle graph.

Animals on the Farm

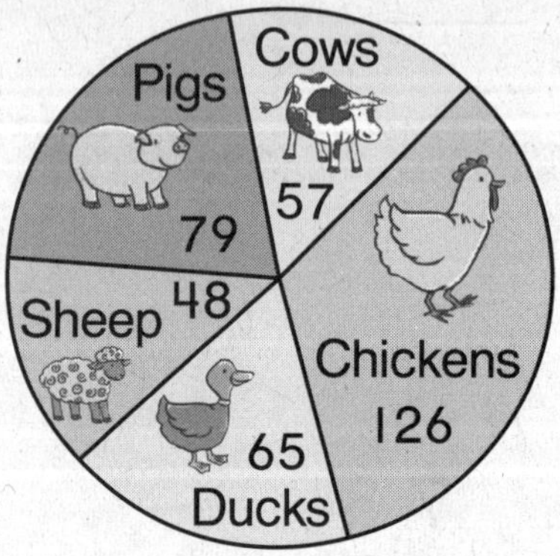

1. How many chickens and ducks are there altogether on the farm?

[ ] ______________ label

2. How many more cows are there than sheep?

[ ] ______________ label

3. How many fewer pigs are there than chickens?

[ ] ______________ label

Subtract.

4. 91 − 52 = ____

5. 87 − 36 = ____

6. 70 − 23 = ____

7. Geometry

Draw one diagonal.	Draw the other diagonal.	Draw both diagonals.
▭	▭	▭

5-7

Name ______

Homework

Solve the story problems. Draw a Proof Drawing if you need to.	Show your work.
1. There were 200 water bottles on a table. The runners in a race took 73 of them. How many water bottles are left on the table? ☐ ______ label	
2. There were 200 weeds in my garden. My little sister pulled out 68 of them. How many weeds are still in the garden? ☐ ______ label	

Subtract.

3. $200 - 66 =$ ______

4. $200 - 82 =$ ______

5. $200 - 68 =$ ______

6. $200 - 95 =$ ______

7. $200 - 72 =$ ______

8. $200 - 47 =$ ______

Name

Targeted Practice

Subtract.

1. $\begin{array}{r} 164 \\ -\ 53 \\ \hline \end{array}$

2. $\begin{array}{r} 136 \\ -\ 73 \\ \hline \end{array}$

3. $\begin{array}{r} 157 \\ -\ 65 \\ \hline \end{array}$

4. $\begin{array}{r} 145 \\ -\ 83 \\ \hline \end{array}$

5. $\begin{array}{r} 187 \\ -\ 44 \\ \hline \end{array}$

6. $\begin{array}{r} 138 \\ -\ 56 \\ \hline \end{array}$

7. $\begin{array}{r} 168 \\ -\ 42 \\ \hline \end{array}$

8. $\begin{array}{r} 123 \\ -\ 61 \\ \hline \end{array}$

9. $\begin{array}{r} 114 \\ -\ 72 \\ \hline \end{array}$

10. $\begin{array}{r} 187 \\ -\ 93 \\ \hline \end{array}$

11. $\begin{array}{r} 199 \\ -\ 88 \\ \hline \end{array}$

12. $\begin{array}{r} 175 \\ -\ 94 \\ \hline \end{array}$

5–8 Name

Homework

Decide if you need to ungroup. Then subtract.

1. $\begin{array}{r} 147 \\ -\ 32 \\ \hline \end{array}$

2. $\begin{array}{r} 147 \\ -\ 38 \\ \hline \end{array}$

3. $\begin{array}{r} 147 \\ -\ 48 \\ \hline \end{array}$

4. $\begin{array}{r} 126 \\ -\ 54 \\ \hline \end{array}$

5. $\begin{array}{r} 126 \\ -\ 57 \\ \hline \end{array}$

6. $\begin{array}{r} 126 \\ -\ 97 \\ \hline \end{array}$

7. $\begin{array}{r} 187 \\ -\ 46 \\ \hline \end{array}$

8. $\begin{array}{r} 187 \\ -\ 49 \\ \hline \end{array}$

9. $\begin{array}{r} 187 \\ -\ 99 \\ \hline \end{array}$

10. $\begin{array}{r} 172 \\ -\ 35 \\ \hline \end{array}$

11. $\begin{array}{r} 172 \\ -\ 85 \\ \hline \end{array}$

12. $\begin{array}{r} 172 \\ -\ 31 \\ \hline \end{array}$

Name ______________________________

Remembering

Solve the story problem. | **Show your work.**

1. The baker made 67 muffins in the morning. He plans to make 93 more. How many muffins will he make if he follows his plan?

☐ ____________________
label

Use the picture graph to answer the questions.

Bikes in the Garage

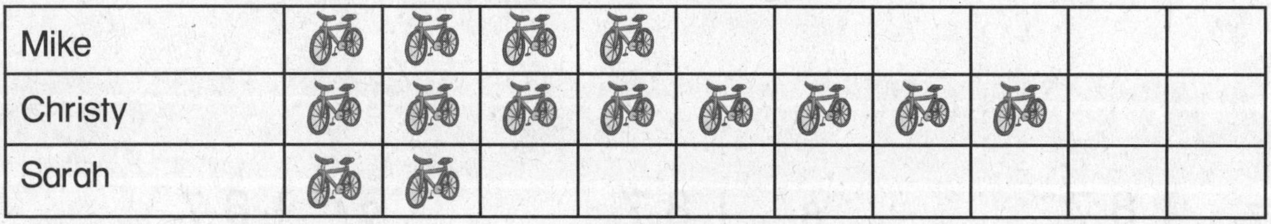

2. How many more bikes does Christy have than Sarah? __________ bikes

3. How many fewer bikes does Sarah have than Mike? __________ bikes

4. Geometry

Connect midpoints of two opposite sides.	Connect midpoints of the other two opposite sides.	Draw both line segments.
☐	☐	☐

5–9 **Name** ____________

Homework

Decide if you need to ungroup. Then subtract.

1.
$$\begin{array}{r} 130 \\ -\ \ 99 \\ \hline \end{array}$$

2.
$$\begin{array}{r} 150 \\ -\ \ 39 \\ \hline \end{array}$$

3.
$$\begin{array}{r} 160 \\ -\ \ 67 \\ \hline \end{array}$$

4.
$$\begin{array}{r} 108 \\ -\ \ 88 \\ \hline \end{array}$$

5.
$$\begin{array}{r} 120 \\ -\ \ 83 \\ \hline \end{array}$$

6.
$$\begin{array}{r} 101 \\ -\ \ 72 \\ \hline \end{array}$$

Solve the story problems.	**Show your work.**
7. There were 120 nickels in a jar. Janice took out 49. How many nickels are in the jar now? ☐ ____________ label	
8. 109 books were sent to the bookstore last Saturday. So far, 25 have been sold. How many have not been sold? ☐ ____________ label	

Name ______________________________

Targeted Practice

Subtract.

1. $\begin{array}{r} 116 \\ -\ 37 \\ \hline \end{array}$

2. $\begin{array}{r} 148 \\ -\ 65 \\ \hline \end{array}$

3. $\begin{array}{r} 176 \\ -\ 89 \\ \hline \end{array}$

4. $\begin{array}{r} 163 \\ -\ 18 \\ \hline \end{array}$

5. $\begin{array}{r} 123 \\ -\ 65 \\ \hline \end{array}$

6. $\begin{array}{r} 104 \\ -\ 12 \\ \hline \end{array}$

7. $\begin{array}{r} 124 \\ -\ 39 \\ \hline \end{array}$

8. $\begin{array}{r} 170 \\ -\ 97 \\ \hline \end{array}$

9. $\begin{array}{r} 133 \\ -\ 35 \\ \hline \end{array}$

10. $\begin{array}{r} 117 \\ -\ 54 \\ \hline \end{array}$

11. $\begin{array}{r} 124 \\ -\ 35 \\ \hline \end{array}$

12. $\begin{array}{r} 146 \\ -\ 17 \\ \hline \end{array}$

5-10

Homework

Name ____________________

What would you like to buy? First, see how much money you have. Pay for the item. How much money will you have left?

Yard Sale

Globe
85¢

Ring
67¢

Sports Bag
98¢

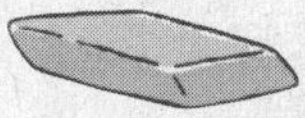

Eraser
79¢

Colored Pencils
66¢

1. I have 124¢ in my pocket.
I bought the ____________________.

$$\begin{array}{r} 124¢ \\ -\quad\quad ¢ \\ \hline \end{array}$$

I have ____________________ ¢ left.

2. I have 152¢ in my pocket.
I bought the ____________________.

$$\begin{array}{r} 152¢ \\ -\quad\quad ¢ \\ \hline \end{array}$$

I have ____________________ ¢ left.

3. I have 145¢ in my pocket.
I bought the ____________________.

$$\begin{array}{r} 145¢ \\ -\quad\quad ¢ \\ \hline \end{array}$$

I have ____________________ ¢ left.

4. I have 131¢ in my pocket.
I bought the ____________________.

$$\begin{array}{r} 131¢ \\ -\quad\quad ¢ \\ \hline \end{array}$$

I have ____________________ ¢ left.

5-10 Name

Remembering

Subtract.

1. 103 − 55 =

2. 150 − 91 =

3. 170 − 93 =

4. 140 − 54 =

5. 109 − 22 =

6. 108 − 49 =

Write the time on the digital clock.

7.

8.

9.

10.

11. Geometry

Draw one diagonal.	Draw the other diagonal.	Draw both diagonals.
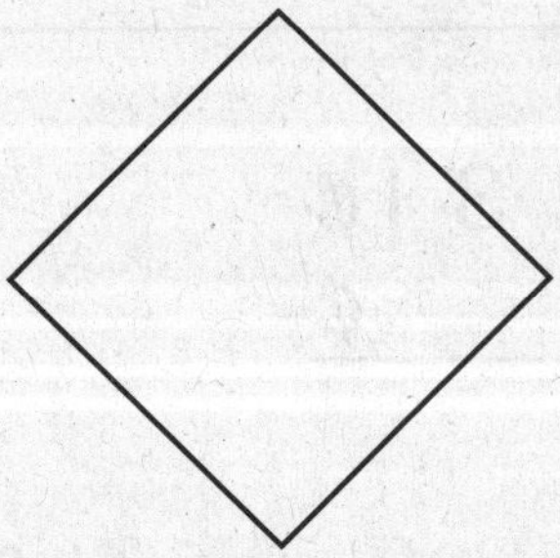	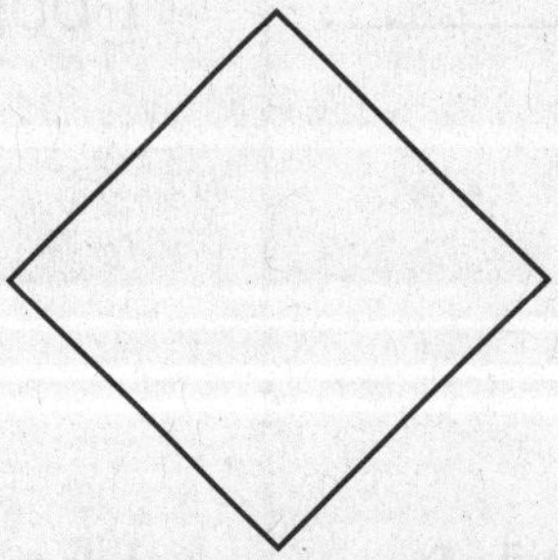	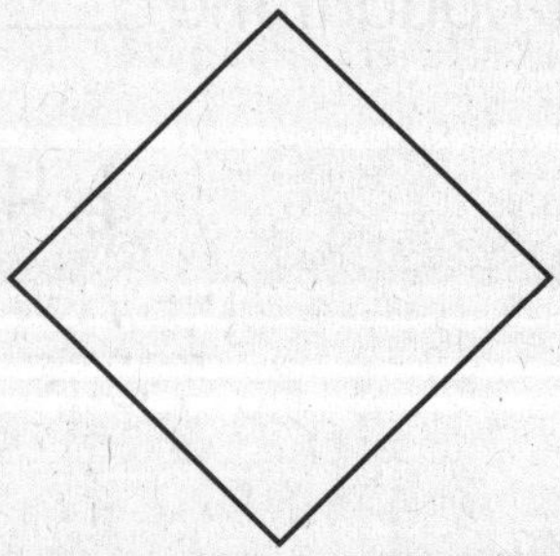

5–11 Name

Homework

Draw a Math Mountain to solve each story problem. Show how you add or subtract.

Show your work.

1. Papi had 148 slices of pizza in his shop. He sold 56 slices. How many slices does Papi have left?

__________ label

2. There were 84 children at the park. Then 61 children joined them. How many children are at the park now?

__________ label

3. Bella had 119 crayons. She gave 36 of them to her friend. How many crayons did she have left?

__________ label

4. Luke ran for 79 minutes. Then he swam for 48 minutes. How many minutes did Luke spend doing these two things?

__________ label

Name

Targeted Practice

Solve the story problems. | **Show your work.**

1. Lena solved a math puzzle in 87 seconds. She solved another puzzle in 63 seconds. How many seconds did it take her to solve both puzzles?

label

2. Lori built a tower with 147 blocks. 59 of the blocks fell off. How many blocks are in the tower now?

label

3. The library owns 113 art books. 74 of them are checked out. How many art books are still in the library?

label

4. My dog Max has 26 spots on him. My other dog, Lucky, has 58 spots on him. How many spots do my dogs have on them?

label

5–12 Name

Homework

1. Write all of the equations for 74, 25, and 49.

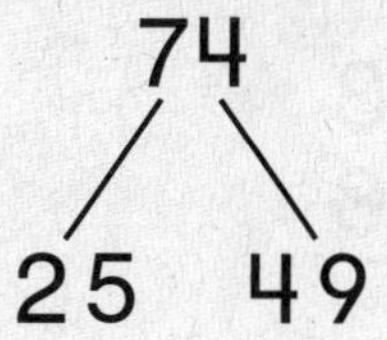

25 + 49 = 74

74 = 25 + 49

2. Write all the equations for 157, 68, and 89.

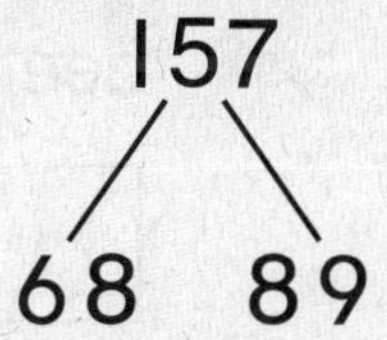

68 + 89 = 157

157 = 68 + 89

Name ____________________

Remembering

Add or subtract.

1.
$$\begin{array}{r} 200 \\ -\ 69 \\ \hline \end{array} \qquad \begin{array}{r} 173 \\ -\ 48 \\ \hline \end{array} \qquad \begin{array}{r} 38 \\ +\ 49 \\ \hline \end{array}$$

Use the information in the bar graph to answer these questions.

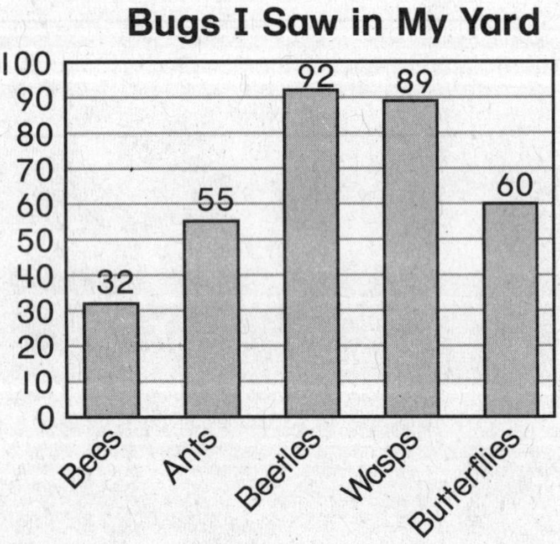

2. How many more butterflies did I see than bees?

☐ ____________ label

3. How many fewer ants did I see than beetles?

☐ ____________ label

4. How many beetles and wasps did I see in my yard?

☐ ____________ label

5. Draw both diagonals.

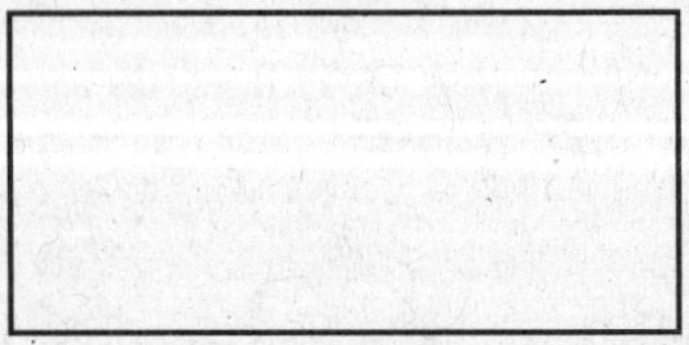

5–13

Name ____________________

Homework

Add or subtract. Watch the sign!

1.
```
  75
+ 28
```

2.
```
  133
-  85
```

3.
```
  47
+ 98
```

4.
```
  87
- 48
```

5.
```
  34
+ 18
```

6.
```
  162
-  84
```

7.
```
  76
+ 93
```

8.
```
  156
-  29
```

9.
```
  58
+ 95
```

10.
```
  121
-  53
```

11.
```
  96
+ 37
```

12.
```
  101
-  39
```

Name ______________________________

Targeted Practice

Solve each story problem. | **Show your work.**

1. The doll shop had 72 new dolls. They sold 34 of them. How many dolls does the shop have left?

[ ] ________ label

2. I collected 95 stickers. My sister collected 48 stickers. How many stickers did my sister and I collect in all?

[ ] ________ label

3. At the dance studio, 67 girls and 86 boys signed up for lessons. In total, how many children signed up for dance lessons?

[ ] ________ label

4. For the picnic, we bought 153 cups. Only 78 of them were used. How many cups are left over?

[ ] ________ label

Name ____________________

Homework

Mr. Green wants to buy some things at a flea market.
He will pay for the items with two dollars (200 cents).
How much change will he get back?

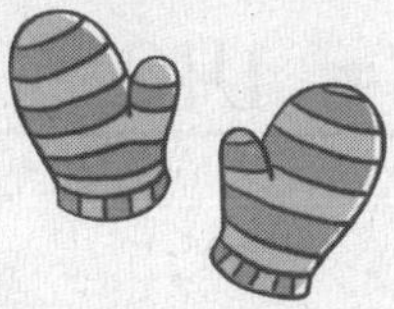

Mittens
57¢

Toy Binoculars
89¢

Toy Camera
96¢

Toy Lamb
78¢

Plant
65¢

1. Mr. Green buys the mittens and the plant.

______ ¢
+ ______ ¢

Total: ______

200¢ − ______ = ______

His change will be ______ ¢.

2. Mr. Green buys the toy lamb and the toy camera.

______ ¢
+ ______ ¢

Total: ______

200¢ − ______ = ______

His change will be ______ ¢.

3. Mr. Green buys the toy binoculars and the toy lamb.

______ ¢
+ ______ ¢

Total: ______

200¢ − ______ = ______

His change will be ______ ¢.

4. Mr. Green buys the toy camera and the plant.

______ ¢
+ ______ ¢

Total: ______

200¢ − ______ = ______

His change will be ______ ¢.

Name ______________________

Remembering

1. Write all of the equations for 142, 58, and 84.

142
58 84

142 = 58 + 84 ______________________

58 + 84 = 142 ______________________

______________________ ______________________

______________________ ______________________

______________________ ______________________

2. What time is it? Write the time on the digital clock.

Solve the story problem. | **Show your work.**

3. In the morning Kevin counted 121 trucks and 53 cars. In the afternoon he counted 68 trucks and 95 cars. How many trucks did he count altogether?

[ ] ______________________
label

Name ______________________

Homework

Add on to solve the story problems.	Show your work.
1. Rudy had 72 ants in his ant farm. He added some more ants. Now there are 209 ants. How many ants did Rudy add? ☐ ________ label	
2. Tina had 92 flowers in her garden this morning. After she took some to school, she had 33 flowers. How many flowers did Tina take to school? ☐ ________ label	
3. Lia collected 119 pins. Then she gave some to Matt. Now Lia has 58 pins. How many pins did Lia give to Matt? ☐ ________ label	
4. There were 124 cars in the garage this morning. Now there are 66 cars in the garage. How many cars left the garage? ☐ ________ label	

Name ______________________________

Targeted Practice

The train stops at the streets shown in the table. Tell the ticket collector where you would like to go. Pay for your ticket with one dollar (100¢). How much money will you get back?

TICKET PRICES

Main Street	38¢
Lincoln Street	46¢
Pleasant Street	57¢
Green Street	63¢
Spring Street	75¢
Newton Street	82¢

Sunshine Line
ONE TICKET
TO: ____________________ STREET
PRICE:

I pay with one dollar.

My change is __________.

Sunshine Line
ONE TICKET
TO: ____________________ STREET
PRICE:

I pay with one dollar.

My change is __________.

Sunshine Line
ONE TICKET
TO: ____________________ STREET
PRICE:

I pay with one dollar.

My change is __________.

Sunshine Line
ONE TICKET
TO: ____________________ STREET
PRICE:

I pay with one dollar.

My change is __________.

5–16

Name ____________________

Homework

Solve the story problems. | **Show your work.**

1. Alma has 129 stars to make a poster. Larry has 82 stars. How many fewer stars does Larry have than Alma?

   [ ] ____________ label

2. The library had 61 magazines. Today they got new magazines. Now there are 135 magazines. How many new magazines did the library get?

   [ ] ____________ label

3. Mori put 209 pretzels in a bowl for her party. Her friends ate some. Now there are 72 pretzels. How many pretzels did her friends eat?

   [ ] ____________ label

4. Eric's hockey team scored 41 goals, and Lou's team scored 110 goals. How many more goals did Lou's team score than Eric's team?

   [ ] ____________ label

Name ______________________

Remembering

Solve the story problem.	Show your work.
1. Al made 163 pickles for the Perfect Pickle contest. The judges ate 74 of them. How many of Al's pickles are left? ☐ ______________ label	

2. Complete the bar graph using the information below.

- Alicia has 5 chores to do.
- Kim has 4 more chores than Alicia.
- Roberto has to finish 2 more chores to have as many chores as Alicia.
- Tyrone has 2 fewer chores than Roberto.

Household Chores

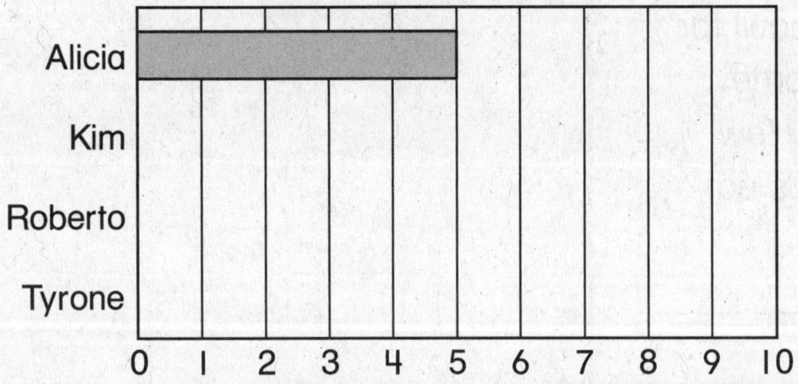

Add.

3. 100 + 83 = ______

10 + 83 = ______

1 + 83 = ______

4. 100 + 6 = ______

10 + 6 = ______

1 + 6 = ______

E–1

Homework

Name ____________________

1. Which two figures are congruent?

Figures ______ and ______ are congruent.

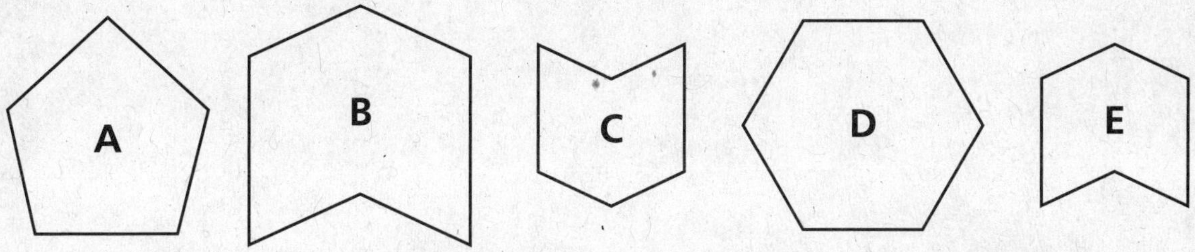

Are the two figures similar? Write *similar* or *not similar*.

2.

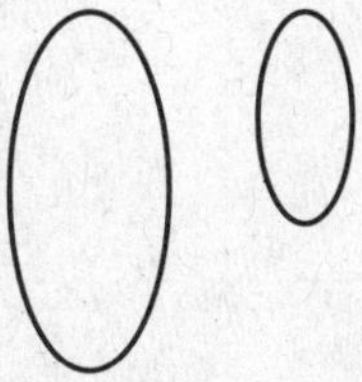

3.

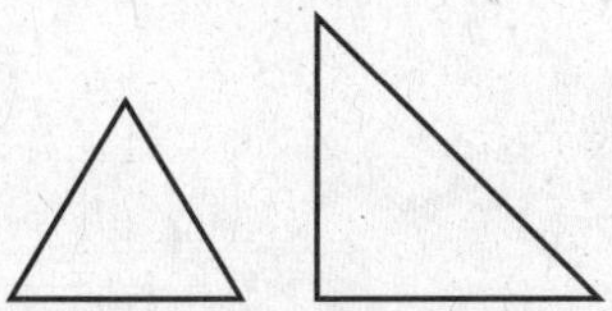

4.

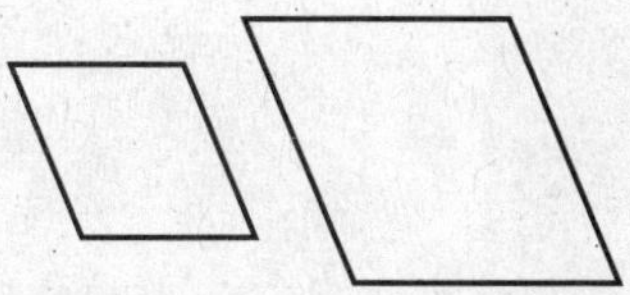

________________ ________________ ________________

5. Sort these shapes into two groups using your own rule.

My sorting rule is ______________________________.

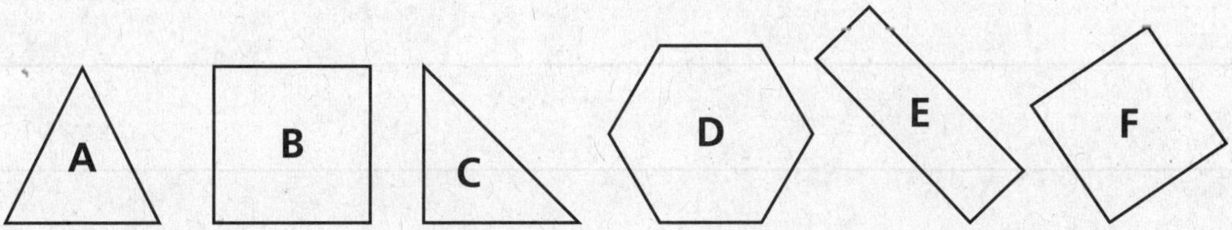

Figures ______________ are ______________________________.

Figures ______________ are ______________________________.

6. On the Back Draw six polygons. Label each with a letter. Describe a sorting rule and sort the figures according to your rule.

Name

E–2

Name ____________________

Homework

Write *slide, flip,* or *turn* to describe how the figure moved.

1. 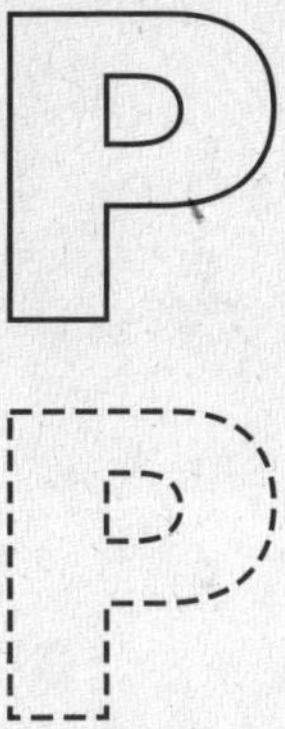

____

2. 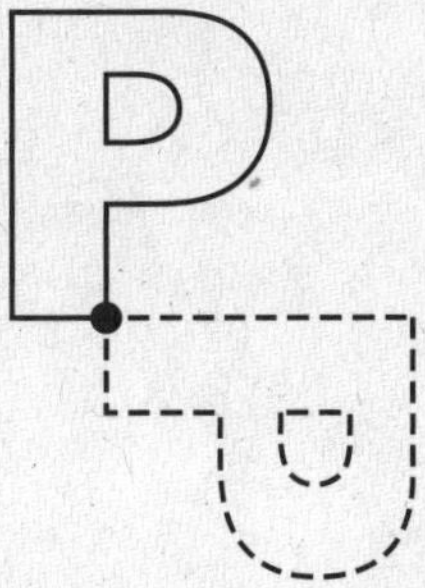

____

3. 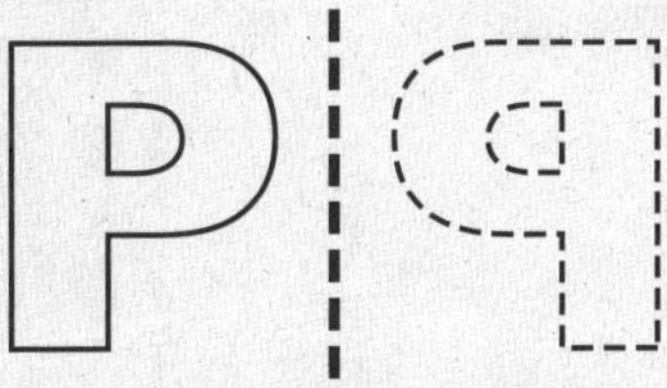

____

4. 

____

Draw the next figure in the pattern.

5.  ______________

6.  ______________

7. **On the Back** Find a flat object in your home and trace it. Slide it to the left and trace it again. Then show a turn using the same object.

Name ______________________________

E-4 Name

Homework

Find the area of each shaded figure in square centimeters.

1.

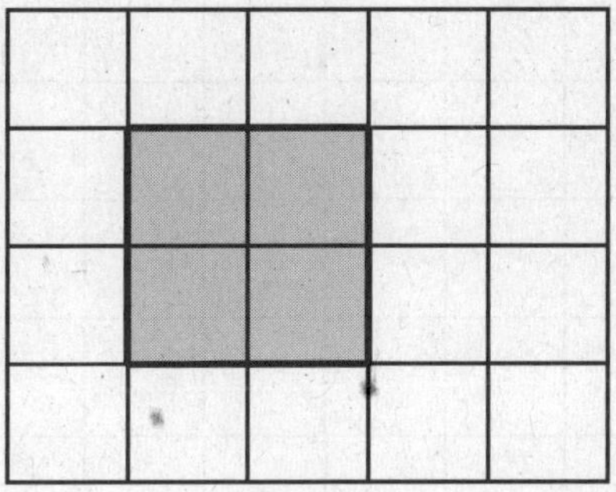

Area = ☐ square centimeters

2.

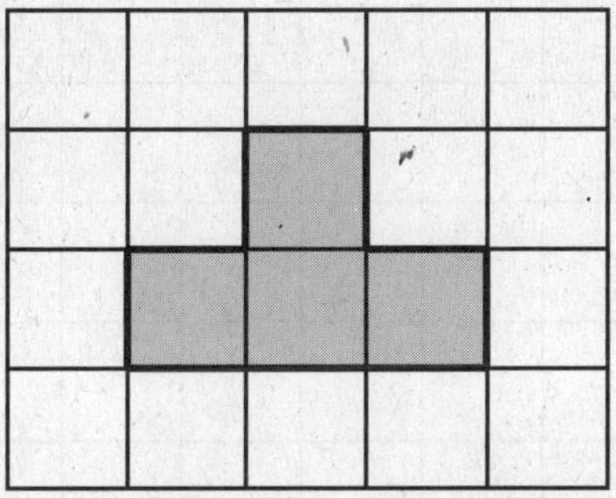

Area = ☐ square centimeters

3.

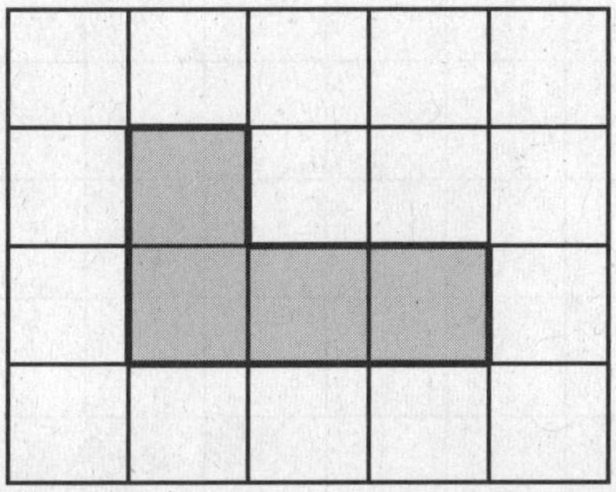

Area = ☐ square centimeters

4.

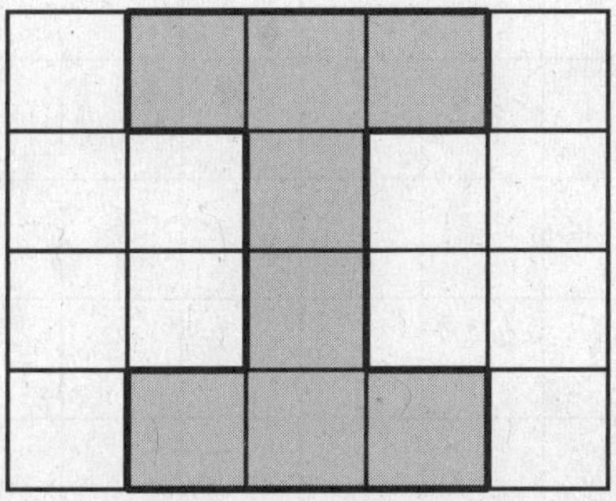

Area = ☐ square centimeters

Estimate the area of each figure in square centimeters.

5.

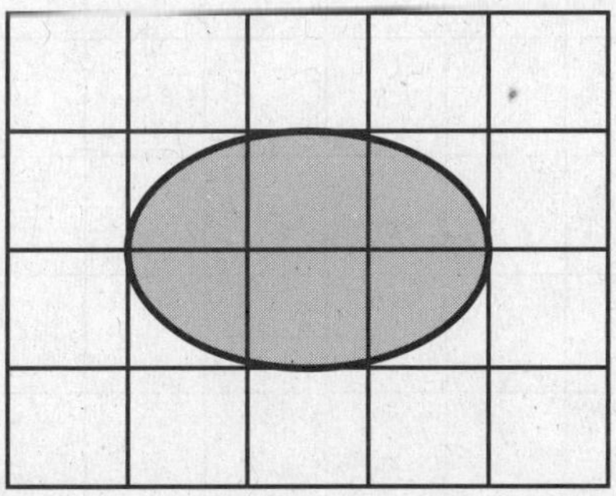

Estimate of area:

☐ square centimeters

6.

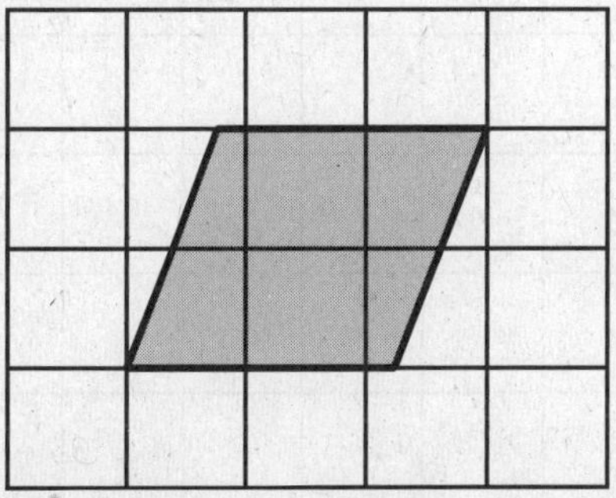

Estimate of area:

☐ square centimeters

7. On the Back Draw three different figures and estimate the area of each in square centimeters.

Name ______________________________

Name ____________________

Homework

Count the hundreds, tens, and ones.
Write the totals.

1. 

_____ Hundreds _____ Tens _____ Ones Total _____

2. 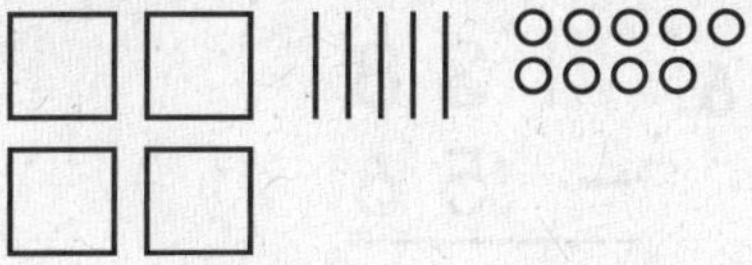

_____ Hundreds _____ Tens _____ Ones Total _____

Draw the hundreds, tens, and ones for the numbers below. Use boxes, sticks, and circles.

3. 2 Hundreds 4 Tens 3 Ones

4. 5 Hundreds 6 Tens 8 Ones

5. 3 Hundreds 8 Tens 2 Ones

6. 1 Hundreds 7 Tens 7 Ones

Name

Targeted Practice

Subtract.

1. $\begin{array}{r} 164 \\ -\ 53 \\ \hline \end{array}$

2. $\begin{array}{r} 136 \\ -\ 73 \\ \hline \end{array}$

3. $\begin{array}{r} 157 \\ -\ 65 \\ \hline \end{array}$

4. $\begin{array}{r} 145 \\ -\ 83 \\ \hline \end{array}$

5. $\begin{array}{r} 187 \\ -\ 44 \\ \hline \end{array}$

6. $\begin{array}{r} 138 \\ -\ 56 \\ \hline \end{array}$

7. $\begin{array}{r} 168 \\ -\ 42 \\ \hline \end{array}$

8. $\begin{array}{r} 123 \\ -\ 61 \\ \hline \end{array}$

9. $\begin{array}{r} 114 \\ -\ 72 \\ \hline \end{array}$

10. $\begin{array}{r} 187 \\ -\ 93 \\ \hline \end{array}$

11. $\begin{array}{r} 199 \\ -\ 88 \\ \hline \end{array}$

12. $\begin{array}{r} 175 \\ -\ 94 \\ \hline \end{array}$

Name ______

Homework

Write the hundreds, tens, and ones.

1. 675 = 600 + 70 + 5
   H T O
2. 519 = ____ + ____ + ____
3. 831 = ____ + ____ + ____
4. 487 = ____ + ____ + ____
5. 222 = ____ + ____ + ____
6. 765 = ____ + ____ + ____

Write the number.

7. 300 + 40 + 6 = 346
   H T O
8. 100 + 60 + 2 = ______
9. 700 + 20 + 4 = ______
10. 200 + 50 + 3 = ______
11. 400 + 70 + 1 = ______
12. 800 + 80 + 8 = ______

Write the missing number. Watch the hundreds, tens, and ones. They are out of order.

13. ____ = 30 + 5 + 400
14. 2 + 80 + 600 = ____
15. ____ = 60 + 800 + 3
16. 900 + 7 + 40 = ____
17. ____ = 300 + 4 + 50
18. 1 + 500 + 70 = ____
19. 729 = 20 + 9 + ____
20. ____ + 6 + 200 = 296

Name ____________________

Remembering

Complete the number sequence. Write the rule.

1. 43, 39, 35, ______, ______, ______ Rule: n ______

2. 66, 69, 72, ______, ______, ______ Rule: n ______

Write the hundreds, tens, and ones.

3. 695 = ______ + ______ + ______

4. 547 = ______ + ______ + ______

Write the number.

5. 400 + 30 + 6 = ______

6. 700 + 80 + 1 = ______

Add ones, tens, or a hundred.

7. 100 + 58 = ______

10 + 58 = ______

1 + 58 = ______

8. 3 + 100 = ______

3 + 10 = ______

3 + 1 = ______

Add or subtract.

9. $\begin{array}{r} 126 \\ -\ 59 \\ \hline \end{array}$

10. $\begin{array}{r} 93 \\ -\ 45 \\ \hline \end{array}$

11. $\begin{array}{r} 78 \\ +\ 67 \\ \hline \end{array}$

12. **Time** On a separate sheet of paper, draw what you do at 8 o'clock in the morning. Show the time on a digital clock.

6–3 **Name** ____________________

Homework

Count by ones. Write the numbers.

1. 396 397 398 399 400 401 402 403 404 405 406

2. 695 696 ___ ___ ___ ___ ___ ___ ___ ___ 705

3. 498 499 ___ ___ ___ ___ ___ ___ ___ ___ 508

4. 894 ___ ___ ___ ___ ___ ___ ___ ___ ___ 904

5. 796 ___ ___ ___ ___ ___ ___ ___ ___ ___ 806

6. 597 ___ ___ ___ ___ ___ ___ ___ ___ ___ 607

Count by tens. Write the numbers.

7. 830 840 850 860 870 880 890 900 910 920 930

8. 470 480 ___ ___ ___ ___ ___ ___ ___ ___ 570

9. 740 ___ ___ ___ ___ ___ ___ ___ ___ ___ 840

10. 380 ___ ___ ___ ___ ___ ___ ___ ___ ___ 480

11. 560 ___ ___ ___ ___ ___ ___ ___ ___ ___ 660

12. 690 ___ ___ ___ ___ ___ ___ ___ ___ ___ 790

Name

Targeted Practice

Subtract.

1. $\begin{array}{r} 110 \\ -\ 47 \\ \hline \end{array}$

2. $\begin{array}{r} 190 \\ -\ 95 \\ \hline \end{array}$

3. $\begin{array}{r} 106 \\ -\ 59 \\ \hline \end{array}$

4. $\begin{array}{r} 107 \\ -\ 68 \\ \hline \end{array}$

5. $\begin{array}{r} 160 \\ -\ 74 \\ \hline \end{array}$

6. $\begin{array}{r} 102 \\ -\ 36 \\ \hline \end{array}$

7. $\begin{array}{r} 140 \\ -\ 68 \\ \hline \end{array}$

8. $\begin{array}{r} 105 \\ -\ 23 \\ \hline \end{array}$

9. $\begin{array}{r} 130 \\ -\ 52 \\ \hline \end{array}$

10. $\begin{array}{r} 103 \\ -\ 98 \\ \hline \end{array}$

11. $\begin{array}{r} 108 \\ -\ 84 \\ \hline \end{array}$

12. $\begin{array}{r} 150 \\ -\ 64 \\ \hline \end{array}$

Name ____________________

Homework

Add or subtract.

1.
$$\begin{array}{r} 46 \\ +\ 97 \\ \hline \end{array}$$

2.
$$\begin{array}{r} 154 \\ -\ 83 \\ \hline \end{array}$$

3.
$$\begin{array}{r} 74 \\ +\ 58 \\ \hline \end{array}$$

Solve each story problem. **Show your work.**

4. You have 100¢ to buy a necklace. The necklace costs 67¢. How much change should you get back?

[ ] ¢

5. Joy caught 47 insects. Ben caught 56. How many insects did the two children catch altogether?

[ ] ____________________ label

6. What number is shown?

____

7. Draw boxes, sticks, and circles to show the number 348.

 Name ____________________

Remembering

Under the coins, write the total amount of money so far.

1. 

____ ____ ____ ____ ____ ____ ____

Use the table to answer the questions.
Fill in the boxes with numbers.
Ring *more* or *fewer*.

Toys

	Toy Trucks	Toy Cars
Molly	85	49
Jake	68	57

2. Jake has ☐ *more* *fewer* toy trucks than Molly has.

3. Molly has ☐ *more* *fewer* toy cars than Jake has.

4. The children have ☐ toy trucks altogether.

Count by ones.

5. 793 794 ____ ____ ____ ____ ____ ____ ____ ____ 803

Count by tens.

6. 840 850 ____ ____ ____ ____ ____ ____ ____ ____ 940

7. Time On a separate sheet of paper, draw what you do at 9 o'clock in the morning. Draw a clock face and show the time.

Name ______

Homework

Solve each story problem.

1. Maria blew up some balloons for a party. She divided them into 4 groups of one hundred and 7 groups of ten. 6 balloons were left over. How many balloons did Maria blow up for the party?

☐ ______ label

2. Roger has 5 erasers. He bought 6 packages of one hundred and 2 packages of ten. How many erasers does Roger have altogether?

☐ ______ label

3. Add.

400 + 200 = ____	440 + 7 = ____	16 + 700 = ____
40 + 50 = ____	84 + 10 = ____	70 + 7 = ____
8 + 460 = ____	200 + 9 = ____	53 + 500 = ____
30 + 10 = ____	60 + 40 = ____	60 + 4 = ____
380 + 10 = ____	900 + 80 = ____	800 + 200 = ____

Name ______________________________

Targeted Practice

Count by ones. Write the numbers.

1. 399 400 401 402 403 404 405 406 407 408 409

2. 596 597 ___ ___ ___ ___ ___ ___ ___ ___ 606

3. 498 499 ___ ___ ___ ___ ___ ___ ___ ___ 508

4. 794 ___ ___ ___ ___ ___ ___ ___ ___ ___ 804

5. 891 ___ ___ ___ ___ ___ ___ ___ ___ ___ 901

6. 597 ___ ___ ___ ___ ___ ___ ___ ___ ___ 607

Count by tens. Write the numbers.

7. 330 340 350 360 370 380 390 400 410 420 430

8. 680 690 ___ ___ ___ ___ ___ ___ ___ ___ 780

9. 820 ___ ___ ___ ___ ___ ___ ___ ___ ___ 920

10. 470 ___ ___ ___ ___ ___ ___ ___ ___ ___ 570

11. 760 ___ ___ ___ ___ ___ ___ ___ ___ ___ 860

12. 690 ___ ___ ___ ___ ___ ___ ___ ___ ___ 790

Name ______________________________

Homework

The quarter machine is broken today. Sometimes it works. Sometimes it doesn't. Write "Yes" if it gave you 25¢. Write "No" if it didn't.

1.

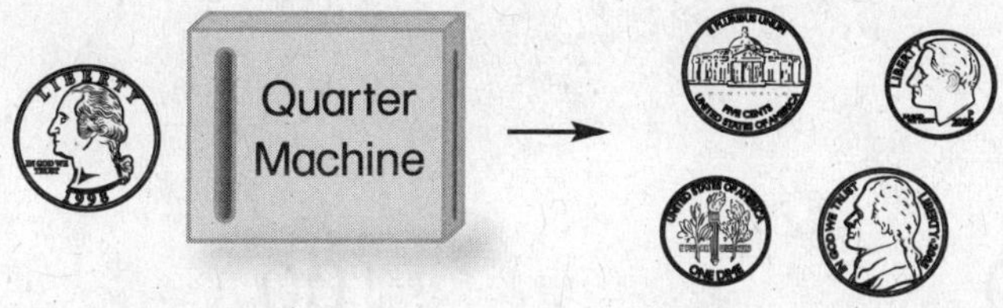

25¢? ______

2.

25¢? ______

3.

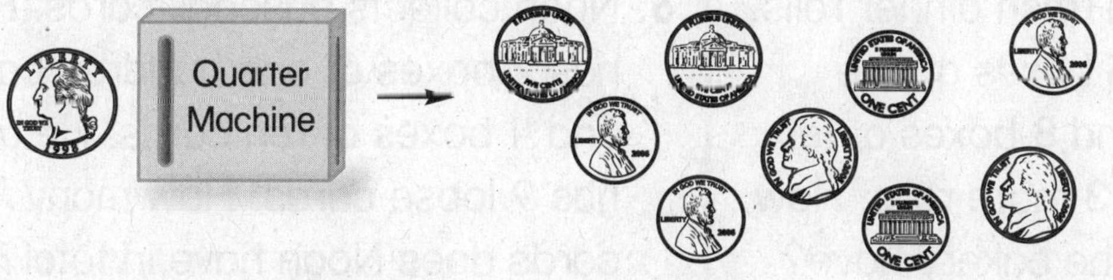

25¢? ______

4.

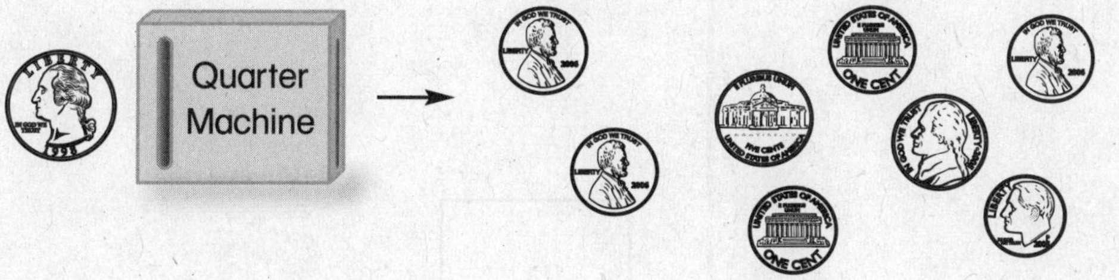

25¢? ______

Name ____________________

Remembering

Add or subtract.

1.

$$\begin{array}{r} 81 \\ +\ 67 \\ \hline \end{array} \qquad \begin{array}{r} 58 \\ +\ 25 \\ \hline \end{array} \qquad \begin{array}{r} 167 \\ -\ 78 \\ \hline \end{array}$$

Find the unknown partner.

2. 100 → 37 and ☐   100 → 89 and ☐   100 → 21 and ☐

Continue the number sequence.

3. 48, 54, 60 ____, ____, ____, ____, ____   Rule: *n* ______

4. 55, 52, 49 ____, ____, ____, ____, ____   Rule: *n* ______

Solve.

5. The bakery had fresh dinner rolls. They counted 5 boxes of one hundred rolls and 8 boxes of ten rolls. They had 3 more rolls. How many rolls did the bakery have?

☐ ____________ label

6. Noah collects baseball cards. He has 2 boxes of one hundred cards and 4 boxes of ten cards. He also has 9 loose cards. How many cards does Noah have in total?

☐ ____________ label

Name ______

Homework

Rewrite these money amounts.

1. 152¢ = $1.52 — 36¢ = ______ — $5.03 = ______

2. $4.86 = 486¢ — 273¢ = ______ — $4.57 = ______

3. $0.06 = ______ — 5¢ = ______ — $3.20 = ______

Count by ones.

4. 26 ___ ___ ___ ___ ___ ___ ___ ___ ___ 36

5. 597 ___ ___ ___ ___ ___ ___ ___ ___ ___ 607

Count by tens.

6. 220 ___ ___ ___ ___ ___ ___ ___ ___ ___ 320

7. 830 ___ ___ ___ ___ ___ ___ ___ ___ ___ 930

Add.

8. $3.96 + $0.08 = $ ___.___

   3¢ + 798¢ = ______¢

   $5.97 + $0.05 = $ ___.___

   494¢ + 9¢ = ______¢

9. $0.09 + $6.93 = $ ___.___

   196¢ + 6¢ = ______¢

   $0.07 + $2.99 = $ ___.___

   894¢ + 8¢ = ______¢

 Name ______________________

Targeted Practice

Count by ones. Write the numbers.

1. 596 597 598 599 600 601 602 603 604 605 606

2. 592 593 ___ ___ ___ ___ ___ ___ ___ ___ 602

3. 895 896 ___ ___ ___ ___ ___ ___ ___ ___ 905

4. 799 ___ ___ ___ ___ ___ ___ ___ ___ ___ 809

5. 491 ___ ___ ___ ___ ___ ___ ___ ___ ___ 501

6. 695 ___ ___ ___ ___ ___ ___ ___ ___ ___ 705

Count by tens. Write the numbers.

7. 630 640 650 660 670 680 690 700 710 720 730

8. 870 880 ___ ___ ___ ___ ___ ___ ___ ___ 970

9. 790 ___ ___ ___ ___ ___ ___ ___ ___ ___ 890

10. 380 ___ ___ ___ ___ ___ ___ ___ ___ ___ 480

11. 550 ___ ___ ___ ___ ___ ___ ___ ___ ___ 650

12. 460 ___ ___ ___ ___ ___ ___ ___ ___ ___ 560

Name ____________________

Homework

Here are some foods from the Grocery Store. The prices are shown too. Answer the questions below.

10 Hot Dogs $2.49 	4 Granola Bars $4.25 	8 Ears of Corn $1.58 
1 Dozen Yogurts $3.22 	2 Bunches of Grapes $0.98 	5 Jars of Pickles $2.13 

How much change would you get from $5.00 if you bought

1. 10 hot dogs? $ 2.51

   $5.00 (regrouped: 4, 9, 10 10) − 2.49 = $2.51 or $5.00 (regrouped: 4 9 10) − 2.49 = $2.51

2. 2 bunches of grapes? $ ___.___

3. 8 ears of corn? $ ___.___

4. 5 jars of pickles? $ ___.___

5. 1 dozen yogurts? $ ___.___

6. 4 granola bars? $ ___.___

Name

Remembering

Use the information in the table to answer the questions.

Sandwiches Sold at the Ballpark

Sandwich	Number Sold
Tuna	18
Peanut Butter	57
Ham	39
Chicken	83
Turkey	26

1. Altogether, how many tuna and turkey sandwiches were sold?

    ____

2. Which three kinds of sandwiches together had the same number sold as chicken?

    ______________,

    ______________, and

    ______________.

3. How many more turkey sandwiches need to be sold to equal the number of ham sandwiches sold? ______________

4. How many more ham sandwiches need to be sold to equal the number of peanut butter sandwiches sold? ______________

5. How many fewer chicken sandwiches would have to be sold to equal the number of tuna sandwiches sold? ______________

6. How many fewer chicken sandwiches would have to be sold to equal the number of turkey sandwiches sold? ______________

Name ______________________________

Homework

Solve each story problem.

1. Rita counts the visitors to the museum. She counted 5 groups of one hundred and 2 groups of ten. She also counted a small group of 7. How many visitors did Rita count?

   ☐ ______________________ label

2. Kay packs buttons at the button factory. She packed 7 boxes of one hundred buttons and 5 boxes of ten. She packed one box of 9 buttons. How many buttons did Kay pack?

   ☐ ______________________ label

Add.

3. 297 + 3 = ______

   7 + 285 = ______

   5 + 143 = ______

   100 + 200 = ______

4. 98 + 9 = ______

   6 + 97 = ______

   45 + 3 = ______

   40 + 30 = ______

5. 38 + 500 = ______

   9 + 300 = ______

   295 + 9 = ______

   50 + 500 = ______

6. 200 + 200 = ______

   11 + 80 = ______

   30 + 410 = ______

   20 + 380 = ______

Name ________________

Targeted Practice

Subtract.

1. $200 - 79$

2. $100 - 48$

3. $200 - 87$

4. $100 - 35$

5. $200 - 51$

6. $100 - 62$

7. $200 - 16$

8. $100 - 24$

9. $200 - 97$

10. $100 - 43$

11. $200 - 58$

12. $100 - 77$

Name ______________________________

Homework

Solve each story problem.

1. Martin sold 58 tickets to the roller coaster ride. He sold 267 tickets to the boat ride. How many tickets did Martin sell?

[ ] ____________ label

2. Justine jumped 485 times on a pogo stick. Then she jumped 329 times when she tried again. How many times did she jump altogether?

[ ] ____________ label

Add.

3. 18 + 549 = [ ]

4. 190 + 89 = [ ]

5. 76 + 570 = [ ]

6. 75 + 656 = [ ]

7. 348 + 162 = [ ]

8. 407 + 394 = [ ]

Name ______________________

Remembering

Complete the number sequence. Write the rule.

1. 84, 86, 88, ________, ________, ________ Rule: *n* ________

2. 52, 46, 40, ________, ________, ________ Rule: *n* ________

3. 21, 29, 37, ________, ________, ________ Rule: *n* ________

How much money is shown here?

4.  = ______¢

5.  = ______¢

Find each unknown partner.

6. 100 → 48 and ☐

7. 100 → 45 and ☐

8. 100 → 24 and ☐

Solve the story problem.	Show your work.
9. The library has 180 CDs in its collection. One morning 28 CDs were checked out. In the afternoon 56 CDs were checked out. How many CDs were not checked out? ☐ ________ label	

Name ______

Homework

Add. Use any method.

1. $2.67
+ $1.56

Make a new ten? ______

Make a new hundred? ______

2. $4.82
+ $3.43

Make a new ten? ______

Make a new hundred? ______

3. $2.75
+ $5.39

Make a new ten? ______

Make a new hundred? ______

4. $6.09
+ $1.88

Make a new ten? ______

Make a new hundred? ______

5. $2.94
+ $4.12

Make a new ten? ______

Make a new hundred? ______

6. $3.07
+ $3.66

Make a new ten? ______

Make a new hundred? ______

Name

Targeted Practice

Solve the story problems.

1. Penny has 596 umbrellas in her store. Kamala has 235 umbrellas in her store. How many umbrellas are in both stores?

label

2. There are 387 rulers in a box. Yesterday, Milo put 113 more rulers in the box. How many rulers are in the box now?

label

3. There are 249 ants crawling up a tree. There are 373 ants on an ant hill. How many ants are there in all?

label

4. Stephanie collected 648 pieces of fabric for a huge quilt. Today, Stephanie added 261 pieces. How many pieces does she have in all?

label

6–12

Homework

Name ____________________

Add. Use any method.

1.
$$\begin{array}{r} 459 \\ +\,267 \\ \hline \end{array}$$

Make a new ten? ______

Make a new hundred? ______

2. 187 + 374 = ______

Make a new ten? ______

Make a new hundred? ______

3.
$$\begin{array}{r} 678 \\ +\,15 \\ \hline \end{array}$$

Make a new ten? ______

Make a new hundred? ______

4. 635 + 92 = ______

Make a new ten? ______

Make a new hundred? ______

5.
$$\begin{array}{r} 389 \\ +\,549 \\ \hline \end{array}$$

Make a new ten? ______

Make a new hundred? ______

6. 64 + 897 = ______

Make a new ten? ______

Make a new hundred? ______

 Name ____________________

Remembering

Find each unknown partner.

1. 100 → 36 and ☐

2. 100 → 43 and ☐

3. 100 → 51 and ☐

Rewrite the money amount. The first one is done for you.

4. 528¢ = $ 5.28

   62¢ = $ 0.62

   $.07 = 7 ¢

5. $1.10 = ____ ¢

   8¢ = $ ____

   $4.90 = ____ ¢

Count by tens.

6. 540 ____ ____ ____ ____ ____ ____ ____ ____ ____ 640

7. 620 ____ ____ ____ ____ ____ ____ ____ ____ ____ 720

Add.

8. $4.98 + $0.05 = $ ____

   5¢ + 799¢ = ____ ¢

   $6.97 + $0.09 = $ ____

   895¢ + 7¢ = ____ ¢

9. $0.07 + $5.94 = $ ____

   292¢ + 9¢ = ____ ¢

   $0.06 + $3.96 = $ ____

   193¢ + 8¢ = ____ ¢

6–13 Name ____________

Homework

Add. Use any method.

1. $$\begin{array}{r} 114 \\ +286 \\ \hline \end{array}$$

Make a new ten? ______

Make a new hundred? ______

2. $$\begin{array}{r} 207 \\ +595 \\ \hline \end{array}$$

Make a new ten? ______

Make a new hundred? ______

3. 68 + 393 = ________

Make a new ten? ______

Make a new hundred? ______

4. 457 + 72 = ________

Make a new ten? ______

Make a new hundred? ______

5. $$\begin{array}{r} 328 \\ +235 \\ \hline \end{array}$$

Make a new ten? ______

Make a new hundred? ______

6. $$\begin{array}{r} 549 \\ +326 \\ \hline \end{array}$$

Make a new ten? ______

Make a new hundred? ______

Name ______

Targeted Practice

Add.

1. $\begin{array}{r} 176 \\ +217 \\ \hline \end{array}$

2. $\begin{array}{r} 347 \\ +242 \\ \hline \end{array}$

3. $\begin{array}{r} 514 \\ +367 \\ \hline \end{array}$

4. $\begin{array}{r} 368 \\ +624 \\ \hline \end{array}$

5. $\begin{array}{r} 224 \\ +374 \\ \hline \end{array}$

6. $\begin{array}{r} 533 \\ +156 \\ \hline \end{array}$

7. $\begin{array}{r} 427 \\ +257 \\ \hline \end{array}$

8. $\begin{array}{r} 314 \\ +569 \\ \hline \end{array}$

9. $\begin{array}{r} 348 \\ +239 \\ \hline \end{array}$

10. $\begin{array}{r} 485 \\ +214 \\ \hline \end{array}$

11. $\begin{array}{r} 124 \\ +566 \\ \hline \end{array}$

12. $\begin{array}{r} 354 \\ +218 \\ \hline \end{array}$

Name ______

Homework

Solve the story problems. Use your favorite method.
Make a Proof Drawing if it helps.

1. Ricardo likes olives. He had 100 olives. He ate 43 of them. How many olives does he have left?

   ☐ ______ label

2. Dawn has 300 pennies in her piggy bank. She gave some to her sister. Now she has 147 left. How many pennies did Dawn give to her sister?

   ☐ ______ label

3. Tory sells hockey sticks to teams in her city. She had 500 and sold 353 to one team. How many hockey sticks does she have left to sell?

   ☐ ______ label

4. Randy collects magnets. Over two years he collected 400 magnets. He collected 125 magnets the first year. How many did he collect the second year?

   ☐ ______ label

Name ______________________________

Remembering

Continue the number sequence.

1. 88, 93, 98 ____, ____, ____, ____, ____ Rule: n ____

   67, 64, 61 ____, ____, ____, ____, ____ Rule: n ____

Add.

2. \$6.92 + \$0.19 = \$______

   14¢ + 388¢ = ______¢

3. \$0.07 + \$2.98 = \$______

   193¢ + 8¢ = ______¢

Write the hundreds, tens, and ones.

4. 837 = ____ + ____ + ____

   902 = ____ + ____ + ____

Write the number.

5. 300 + 40 + 8 = ______

   500 + 20 + 0 = ______

Count by tens.

6. 420 ___ ___ ___ ___ ___ ___ ___ ___ ___ 520

7. 650 ___ ___ ___ ___ ___ ___ ___ ___ ___ 750

Find each unknown partner.

8. 100: 22 and ☐   100: 79 and ☐   100: 87 and ☐

6–15 Name ______

Homework

Decide if you need to ungroup. If you need to ungroup, draw a magnifying glass around the top number. Then find the answer.

1.
$$\begin{array}{r} 730 \\ -499 \\ \hline \end{array}$$

Ungroup to get 10 ones? ______

Ungroup to get 10 tens? ______

2.
$$\begin{array}{r} 950 \\ -639 \\ \hline \end{array}$$

Ungroup to get 10 ones? ______

Ungroup to get 10 tens? ______

3.
$$\begin{array}{r} 300 \\ -167 \\ \hline \end{array}$$

Ungroup to get 10 ones? ______

Ungroup to get 10 tens? ______

4.
$$\begin{array}{r} 404 \\ -188 \\ \hline \end{array}$$

Ungroup to get 10 ones? ______

Ungroup to get 10 tens? ______

5.
$$\begin{array}{r} 420 \\ -183 \\ \hline \end{array}$$

Ungroup to get 10 ones? ______

Ungroup to get 10 tens? ______

6. $502 - 149 =$ ______

Ungroup to get 10 ones? ______

Ungroup to get 10 tens? ______

Name ______

Targeted Practice

Add.

1. $\begin{array}{r} 226 \\ +\ 457 \\ \hline \end{array}$

2. $\begin{array}{r} 547 \\ +\ 332 \\ \hline \end{array}$

3. $\begin{array}{r} 424 \\ +\ 357 \\ \hline \end{array}$

4. $\begin{array}{r} 458 \\ +\ 214 \\ \hline \end{array}$

5. $\begin{array}{r} 114 \\ +\ 874 \\ \hline \end{array}$

6. $\begin{array}{r} 623 \\ +\ 256 \\ \hline \end{array}$

7. $\begin{array}{r} 537 \\ +\ 457 \\ \hline \end{array}$

8. $\begin{array}{r} 424 \\ +\ 269 \\ \hline \end{array}$

9. $\begin{array}{r} 458 \\ +\ 439 \\ \hline \end{array}$

10. $\begin{array}{r} 575 \\ +\ 324 \\ \hline \end{array}$

11. $\begin{array}{r} 234 \\ +\ 456 \\ \hline \end{array}$

12. $\begin{array}{r} 438 \\ +\ 329 \\ \hline \end{array}$

6–16

Name ______________________________

Homework

Decide if you need to ungroup. If you need to ungroup, draw a magnifying glass around the top number. Then find the answer.

1.
```
  $4.0 8
– $0.5 3
```
Ungroup to get 10 ones? ______

Ungroup to get 10 tens? ______

2.
```
  $7.1 0
– $2.2 8
```
Ungroup to get 10 ones? ______

Ungroup to get 10 tens? ______

3.
```
  $3.0 0
– $2.6 8
```
Ungroup to get 10 ones? ______

Ungroup to get 10 tens? ______

4.
```
  $2.0 7
– $0.5 5
```
Ungroup to get 10 ones? ______

Ungroup to get 10 tens? ______

5.
```
  $5.9 0
– $1.7 7
```
Ungroup to get 10 ones? ______

Ungroup to get 10 tens? ______

6.
```
  $9.0 3
– $6.3 3
```
Ungroup to get 10 ones? ______

Ungroup to get 10 tens? ______

 Name ____________________

Remembering

How much money is shown here?

1.  = ________ ¢

Add or subtract.

2.
```
  375
+ 246
-----
```

3.
```
  546
+ 262
-----
```

4.
```
  151
-  82
-----
```

5.
```
  118
-  65
-----
```

Complete the number sequence. Write the rule.

6. 11, 17, 23, ________, ________, ________ Rule: *n* ________

Write 8 equations for each Math Mountain.

7.
```
    223
   /   \
 91     132
```

________________ ________________

________________ ________________

________________ ________________

________________ ________________

Subtract.

8.
```
  400
-  34
-----
```

9.
```
  630
-  59
-----
```

10.
```
  701
-  93
-----
```

11.
```
  226
-  37
-----
```

Name ________________

Homework

Decide if you need to ungroup. If you need to ungroup, draw a magnifying glass around the top number. Then find the answer.

1.
$$\begin{array}{r} 531 \\ -\,434 \\ \hline \end{array}$$

Ungroup to get 10 ones? ______

Ungroup to get 10 tens? ______

2.
$$\begin{array}{r} 579 \\ -\,296 \\ \hline \end{array}$$

Ungroup to get 10 ones? ______

Ungroup to get 10 tens? ______

3.
$$\begin{array}{r} 391 \\ -\,265 \\ \hline \end{array}$$

Ungroup to get 10 ones? ______

Ungroup to get 10 tens? ______

4. 238 − 177 = ______

Ungroup to get 10 ones? ______

Ungroup to get 10 tens? ______

5. Latoya plans to drive 572 miles on her vacation. The first day she drove 386 miles. How many more miles does she have to drive?

☐ ______________
label

6. Elena had $7.35. She bought a gift for $4.27. How much money does she have left?

☐

Name ______________________________

Targeted Practice

Solve each story problem.

1. Carrie has 654 stamps in her stamp collection. Hector has 327 stamps in his collection. How many stamps are there in both collections?

☐ ______________ label

2. In one week, Farida drove her motorcycle 569 miles. The next week she drove 253 miles. How many miles did she drive in the two weeks?

☐ ______________ label

3. Kuri has read 369 pages in her book. This weekend, Kuri plans to read 252 pages. How many pages will Kuri have read at the end of this weekend?

☐ ______________ label

4. Armani has saved up 283 dollars. Lita has saved up 327 dollars. How much money do Armani and Lita have together?

☐ ______________ label

6–18 Name ____________________

Homework

Decide if you need to ungroup. If you need to ungroup, draw a magnifying glass around the top number. Then find the answer.

1.
$$\begin{array}{r} 630 \\ -\ 318 \\ \hline \end{array}$$

Ungroup to get 10 ones? ______

Ungroup to get 10 tens? ______

2.
$$\begin{array}{r} 931 \\ -\ 845 \\ \hline \end{array}$$

Ungroup to get 10 ones? ______

Ungroup to get 10 tens? ______

3.
$$\begin{array}{r} 407 \\ -\ 274 \\ \hline \end{array}$$

Ungroup to get 10 ones? ______

Ungroup to get 10 tens? ______

4.
$$\begin{array}{r} 498 \\ -\ 276 \\ \hline \end{array}$$

Ungroup to get 10 ones? ______

Ungroup to get 10 tens? ______

5. Jamal had 590 craft sticks. He used 413 craft sticks to make a building. How many craft sticks does he have left?

[   ] ______________
label

6. Clare and her family are driving to Blue Valley Mountains. Blue Valley Mountains is 290 miles from their home. They drove 184 miles. How many more miles do they have to go?

[   ] ______________
label

Name ____________________

Remembering

Complete the money tables.

1.

49¢		
Q		= ¢
D	1	= 10¢
N		= ¢
P		= ¢
		¢

2.

72¢		
Q	2	= 50¢
D		= ¢
N		= ¢
P	2	= ¢
		¢

3.

65¢		
Q		= ¢
D		= ¢
N		= ¢
P	0	= 0¢
		¢

The market sells fresh fruit. The table shows how much fruit they sold this week.

Fresh Fruit Sold This Week

Lemons	200
Apples	680
Bananas	450

4. How many fewer lemons did the market sell than bananas?

____

5. How many more apples did the market sell than bananas?

____

6. How many fewer lemons did the market sell than apples?

____

7. Time On a separate piece of paper, draw what you do at 10 o'clock P.M. Show the time on a digital clock.

Name ____________________

Homework

Decide if you need to add or subtract. Then solve each problem.

1.
```
  184
+ 433
-----
```

2.
```
  552
- 399
-----
```

3.
```
  328
- 119
-----
```

4.
```
  288
+ 294
-----
```

5. 967 − 548 = ______

6. 474 − 355 = ______

Name

Targeted Practice

Subtract.

1. $\begin{array}{r} 391 \\ -265 \\ \hline \end{array}$

2. $\begin{array}{r} 648 \\ -156 \\ \hline \end{array}$

3. $\begin{array}{r} 925 \\ -583 \\ \hline \end{array}$

4. $\begin{array}{r} 362 \\ -171 \\ \hline \end{array}$

5. $\begin{array}{r} 652 \\ -234 \\ \hline \end{array}$

6. $\begin{array}{r} 774 \\ -258 \\ \hline \end{array}$

Name ______________________________

Homework

Solve each story problem.

1. Abigail's mother gave her some carrots to sell at the state fair. Then Abigail picked 367 more from the garden. Now Abigail has 825 carrots to sell. How many did her mother give her?

   [ ] ______________ label

2. Stanley the grocer had lots of mushrooms. He sold 679 in the morning. Now he has 244 left to sell. How many mushrooms did Stanley have at the beginning?

   [ ] ______________ label

3. Carmen has 347 guppies in her fish tank. Peter must give away 156 of his guppies to have the same number as Carmen. How many guppies does Peter have in his tank?

   [ ] ______________ label

4. Stanley bought 283 bags of flour for his store. Ted needs 148 bags of flour to have as many as Stanley. How many bags of flour does Ted have?

   [ ] ______________ label

 Name

Remembering

Add or subtract.

1. $\begin{array}{r} 504 \\ +399 \\ \hline \end{array}$ $\begin{array}{r} 962 \\ -775 \\ \hline \end{array}$ $\begin{array}{r} \$4.73 \\ -\$2.58 \\ \hline \end{array}$

Write the hundreds, tens, and ones.

2. 382 = ______ + ______ + ______

   738 = ______ + ______ + ______

Write the number.

3. 90 + 0 + 400 = ______

   6 + 500 + 10 = ______

Solve each story problem.

4. 198 people are already on an airplane. The rest are waiting to get on. There are 347 people altogether. How many people are waiting to get on the airplane?

   ☐ ______________ label

5. Colby is practicing football. He kicked the ball 168 times this morning. He kicked the ball 207 times this afternoon. How many times did he kick today?

   ☐ ______________ label

6. **Time** On a separate piece of paper, draw what you do at 6 o'clock in the morning. Draw a clock face and show the time.

Name

Homework

Solve each story problem.

1. Mario bought 644 plastic cups. He gave 337 to the art teacher. How many cups did he have left?

   label

2. Joel collects baseball cards. He had 568 cards. Then he bought 329 more at a yard sale. How many cards does he have now?

   label

3. A bird collected 392 sticks to build a nest. Then she collected 165 more. How many sticks did the bird collect?

   label

4. There are 765 books in the school library. 259 are paperback, and the rest are hardcover. How many hardcover books are there in the library?

   label

Name

Targeted Practice

Solve each story problem.

1. Some children had 458 raisins. They got hungry and ate some of them. Now they have 285 left. How many raisins did they eat?

label

2. Tom collects rocks. Last night, he went to the beach and found 329 rocks. This morning he found 468 rocks. How many rocks did he find altogether?

label

3. Sarah had 285 cherries. Then she bought 364 more cherries. How many total cherries does she have now?

label

4. Noella has 563 marbles. Soniah has 255. How many more marbles does Noella have than Soniah?

label

Name ____________________

Homework

Directions for the puzzle appearing on page 242.

1. Start by coloring in the 7 dotted squares. These are "free" squares. They are part of the puzzle solution.
2. Solve a problem below. Then look for the answer in the puzzle grid. Color in that puzzle piece.
3. Solve all 17 problems correctly. Color in the puzzle pieces for all 17 correct answers.
4. Name the hidden picture. It is a(n) ______________.

$$\begin{array}{r} 533 \\ +288 \\ \hline \end{array} \quad \begin{array}{r} 746 \\ -517 \\ \hline \end{array} \quad \begin{array}{r} 675 \\ +249 \\ \hline \end{array} \quad \begin{array}{r} 854 \\ -437 \\ \hline \end{array}$$

$$\begin{array}{r} 662 \\ -398 \\ \hline \end{array} \quad \begin{array}{r} 717 \\ +175 \\ \hline \end{array} \quad \begin{array}{r} 808 \\ -232 \\ \hline \end{array} \quad \begin{array}{r} 453 \\ +390 \\ \hline \end{array}$$

$$\begin{array}{r} 689 \\ +129 \\ \hline \end{array} \quad \begin{array}{r} 926 \\ -843 \\ \hline \end{array} \quad \begin{array}{r} 591 \\ +349 \\ \hline \end{array} \quad \begin{array}{r} 580 \\ -445 \\ \hline \end{array}$$

$$\begin{array}{r} 813 \\ -116 \\ \hline \end{array} \quad \begin{array}{r} 386 \\ +371 \\ \hline \end{array} \quad \begin{array}{r} 754 \\ -469 \\ \hline \end{array} \quad \begin{array}{r} 574 \\ +209 \\ \hline \end{array} \quad \begin{array}{r} 372 \\ -187 \\ \hline \end{array}$$

Name ____________________

Homework

See page 241 for directions on how to solve the puzzle.

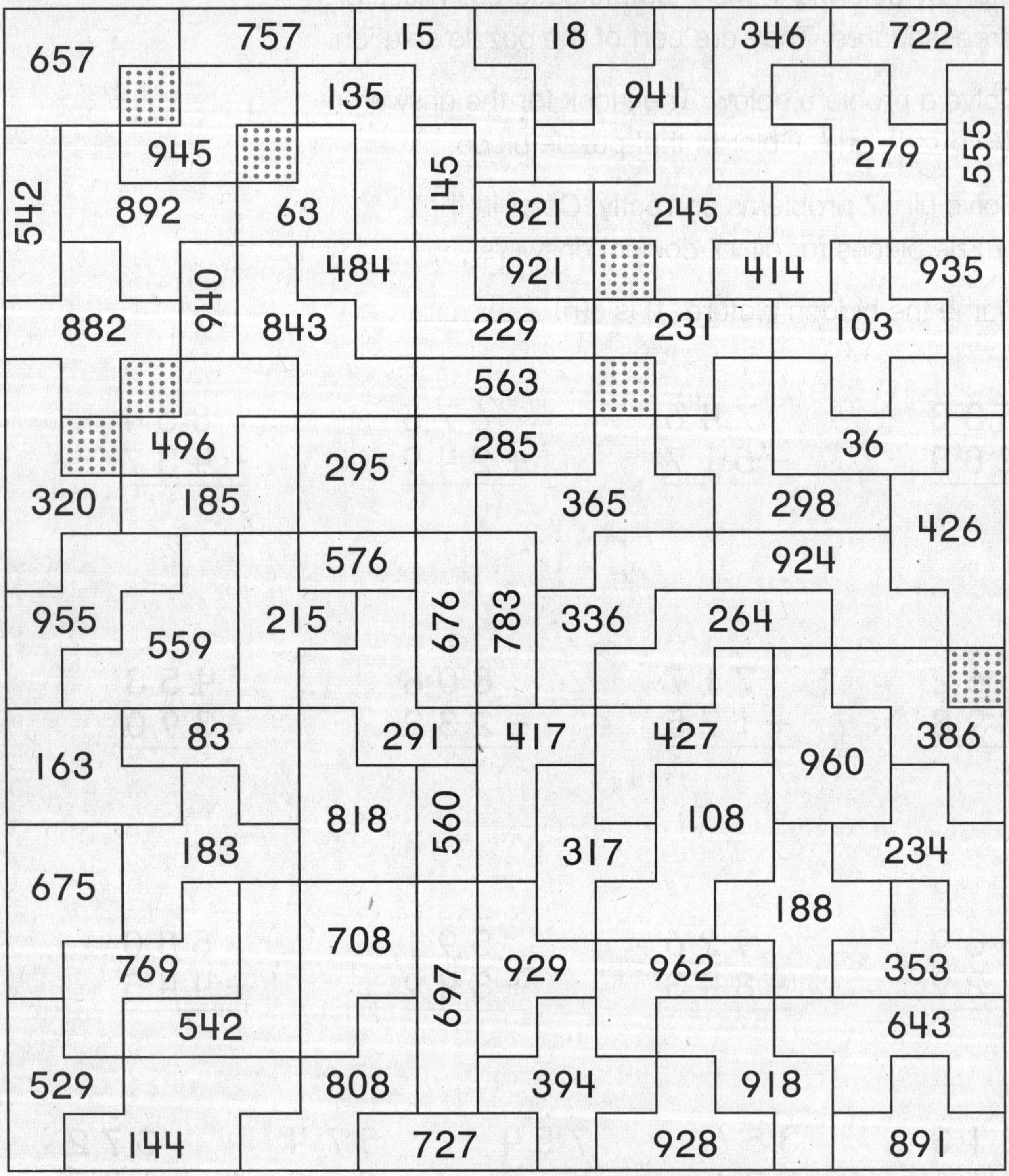

F–1 **Homework**

Name ____________________

1. Complete the table. Estimate the height of six people, pets, or objects. Find the actual heights. If necessary, round measurements to the nearest centimeter. Then, calculate the difference between your estimate and the actual measurement.

Person, pet, or object	Estimated height in cm	Actual height in cm	Difference between estimated and actual height in cm

2. On the Back Write two questions about the data you collected. Answer your questions.

Name

F–2 Name ______________________________

Homework

Measure four rectangular objects using your paper meter stick. Include at least two objects that have measurements greater than 100 cm. Write a clue for each object about its color, shape, location, or use. Ask your Homework Helper to guess each of your objects.

1. The length of the object is ____________ cm.

   The width of the object is ____________ cm.

   Clue: ____

   ____

2. The length of the object is ____________ cm.

   The width of the object is ____________ cm.

   Clue: ____

   ____

3. The length of the object is ____________ cm.

   The width of the object is ____________ cm.

   Clue: ____

   ____

4. The length of the object is ____________ cm.

   The width of the object is ____________ cm.

   Clue: ____

   ____

5. **On the Back** Use your paper meter stick to measure the height of one or more people in your family. Make a list with the name of each family member and his or her height.

Name

F–3

Name ____________________

Homework

Solve the story problems. Ring *yes* or *no*.	**Show your work.**
1. The height of the window in Juan's bedroom is 2 m 3 dm. Juan found some curtains that are 203 cm long. Are the curtains long enough? Yes No Why or why not? ____________________ ____________________	
2. Max needs $2.50 to buy birthday cards for his twin cousins. He has 1 dollar, 9 dimes, and 7 pennies. Does he have enough money? Yes No Why or why not? ____________________ ____________________	
3. Jack says that he is taller than Taci. Jack is 11 dm 3 cm tall. Taci is 1 m 1 dm tall. Is Jack taller than Taci? Yes No Why or why not? ____________________ ____________________	

4. On the Back Measure three objects, each with a length greater than 100 cm. Write each length measurement in centimeters. Then, write the equivalent measurements in meters, decimeters, and centimeters.

Name

F-4 **Name** ______

Homework

1. Answer each question. Draw a picture if it helps.

How many dimes in 2 dollars? ______

How many pennies in 3 dimes? ______

How many ones in 2 tens? ______

How many tens in 2 hundreds? ______

How many decimeters in 2 m? ______

How many centimeters in 2 m? ______

How many pennies in 3 dollars? ______

How many ones in 4 tens? ______

2. Write the numbers.

3 m 4 dm 7 cm = ______ dm 7 cm = ______ cm	____ m ____ dm ____ cm = 36 dm 4 cm = ______ cm	____ m ____ dm ____ cm = 65 dm 6 cm = ______ cm
2 m 7 dm 1 cm = ______ dm 1 cm = ______ cm	____ m ____ dm ____ cm = 43 dm 8 cm = ______ cm	$2.48 = ____ dimes ____ pennies = ______ pennies

$6.10 = ____ dimes ____ pennies = ______ pennies	$____.______ = ____ dimes ____ pennies = 325 pennies

3. On the Back Draw a line segment 10 cm long. Label its length in decimeters. Draw another line segment 2 dm long. Label its length in centimeters.

Name

F–5

Name ______________________________

Homework

Is each shape two-dimensional (2-D) or three-dimensional (3-D)?

1. 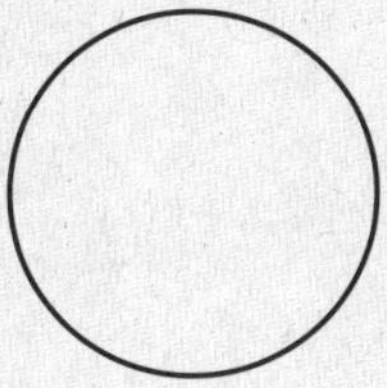

____

2. 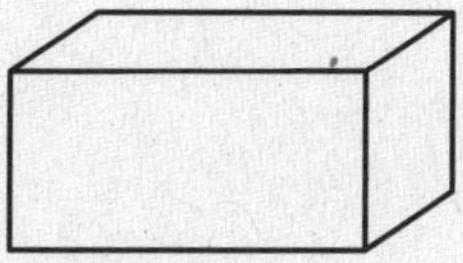

____

3. 

____

For each rectangular prism, draw the top view, front view, and side views.

4. 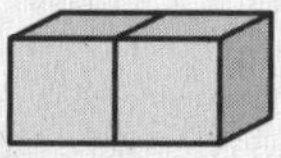

top	front	side

5. 

top	front	side

Find the volume of each three-dimensional shape.

6. 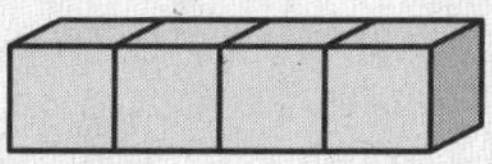

________ cubic units

7. 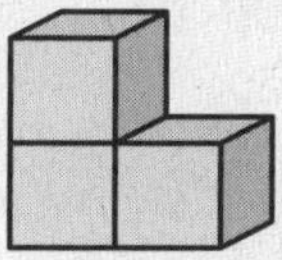

________ cubic units

8. 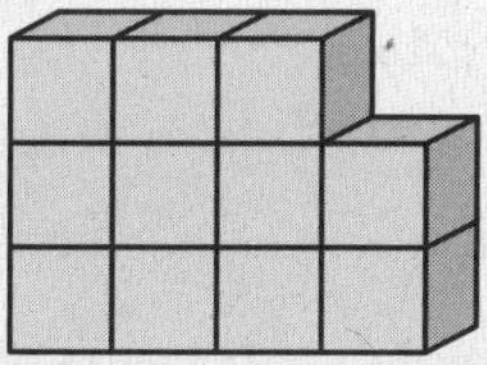

________ cubic units

9. On the Back Find a rectangular prism in your home. Trace or draw the top, front, and side views.

Name

F–6 Name ______________________________

Homework

1. Describe how the pair of shapes is alike and different.

Shapes	How these shapes are alike	How these shapes are different
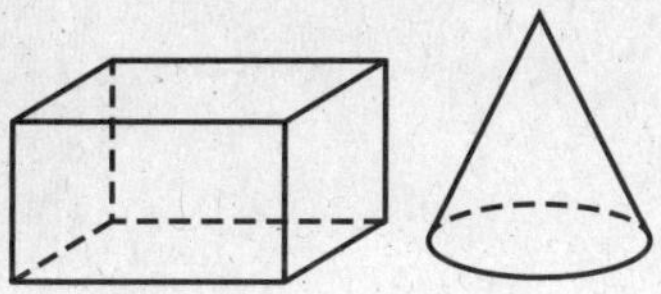		

cube | sphere | cylinder | cone | rectangular prism | square pyramid

2. Use a Venn diagram to sort these shapes into two groups: shapes that stack and shapes that slide. Write the names of the shapes in the Venn diagram.

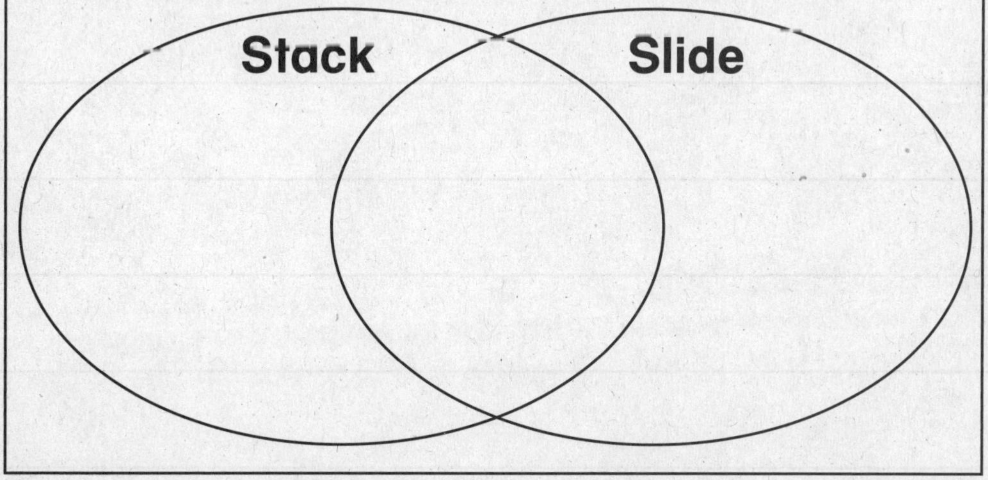

3. On the Back Find three-dimensional shapes in your home and neighborhood. Draw the objects you find and describe what they are used for.

Name

7–1

Name ______

Homework

Count by 2s. Then multiply.

1. Horns on a bull

2 4 6 8 $4 \times 2 =$ 8

2. Eyes on a teddy bear

____ ____ $2 \times 2 =$ ____

3. Hearts on a valentine

____ ____ ____ ____ ____ ____ $6 \times 2 =$ ____

4. Leaves on a holly branch

____ ____ ____ ____ ____ ____ ____ ____ ____ $9 \times 2 =$ ____

5. Wheels on a bicycle

____ ____ ____ ____ ____ $5 \times 2 =$ ____

Name ______

Targeted Practice

Subtract. Ungroup if you need to.

1. $\begin{array}{r} 592 \\ -475 \\ \hline \end{array}$

2. $\begin{array}{r} 635 \\ -464 \\ \hline \end{array}$

3. $\begin{array}{r} 417 \\ -246 \\ \hline \end{array}$

4. $\begin{array}{r} 773 \\ -527 \\ \hline \end{array}$

5. 846 − 584 = ______

6. 934 − 417 = ______

Name ______________________

Homework

Count by 3s. Then multiply.

1. Flowers on a stem

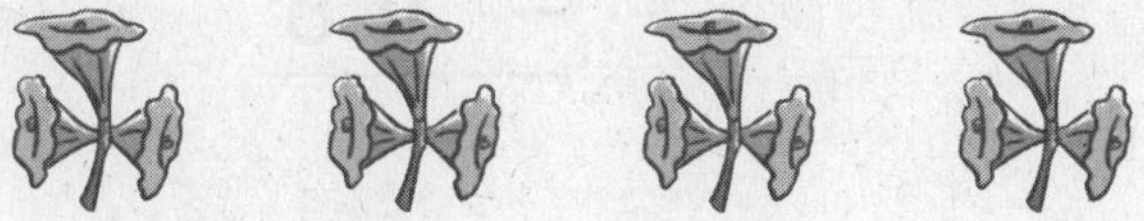

3 ___ 6 ___ 9 ___ 12 ___

$4 \times 3 =$ 12

2. Strawberries on a plate

_____ _____ _____

$3 \times 3 =$ _____

3. Sides in triangles

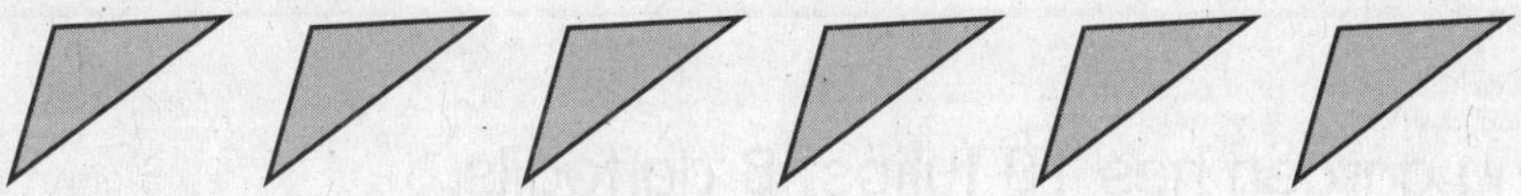

_____ _____ _____ _____ _____ _____

$6 \times 3 =$ _____

4. Crayons in a group

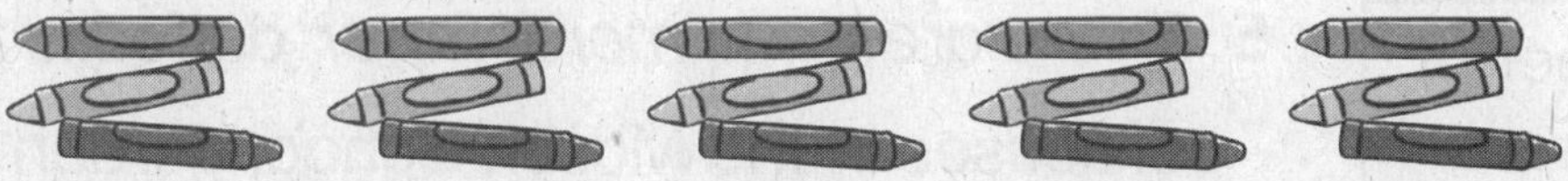

_____ _____ _____ _____ _____

$5 \times 3 =$ _____

5. Toys in a sandbox play set

_____ _____ _____ _____ _____ _____ _____

$7 \times 3 =$ _____

7–2 Name ______

Remembering

Add or subtract.

1. $\begin{array}{r} 415 \\ +191 \\ \hline \end{array}$

2. $\begin{array}{r} 754 \\ +187 \\ \hline \end{array}$

3. $\begin{array}{r} 501 \\ -\ 48 \\ \hline \end{array}$

Solve the story problems.	Show your work.
4. There are 5 trucks. Each truck has 2 logs in it. How many logs are there altogether? 2 + 2 + 2 + 2 + 2 = ______ 5 × 2 = ______ ☐ ______ label	

The Mason School spring garden has 10 tulips, 8 daffodils, 11 crocuses, and 6 snowdrops. Make a table to show this. Then answer the questions. Ring *more* or *fewer*.

______

	Number of Flowers

5. There are ☐ *more fewer* daffodils than crocuses in the Mason School garden.

6. There are ☐ *more fewer* tulips than daffodils in the Mason School garden.

7. The school needs to plant ☐ more snowdrops to have as many as there are tulips.

7–3

Name ____________________

Homework

Count by 4s. Then multiply.

1. Wings on a dragonfly

4 8 12 16 20 $5 \times 4 =$ 20

2. Sides on a rectangle

____ ____ ____ ____ ____ ____ $6 \times 4 =$ ____

3. Legs on a giraffe

____ ____ ____ ____ $4 \times 4 =$ ____

4. Fish in a frying pan

____ ____ ____ ____ ____ $5 \times 4 =$ ____

5. Apples on a plate

____ ____ ____ ____ ____ ____ ____ ____ $8 \times 4 =$ ____

Name

Targeted Practice

Subtract.

1.
$$\begin{array}{r} 724 \\ -\,358 \\ \hline \end{array}$$

2.
$$\begin{array}{r} 642 \\ -\,293 \\ \hline \end{array}$$

3.
$$\begin{array}{r} 663 \\ -\,474 \\ \hline \end{array}$$

4.
$$\begin{array}{r} 972 \\ -\,389 \\ \hline \end{array}$$

5.
$$\begin{array}{r} 842 \\ -\,567 \\ \hline \end{array}$$

6.
$$\begin{array}{r} \$5.25 \\ -\,\$2.38 \\ \hline \end{array}$$

Name ____________________

Homework

Count by 5s. Then multiply.

1. Peas in a peapod

____ ____ ____ ____ $4 \times 5 =$ ____

2. Arms on a starfish

____ ____ ____ ____ ____ ____ ____ ____ ____

$9 \times 5 =$ ____

3. Leaves on a branch

____ ____ ____ ____ ____ ____ ____ $7 \times 5 =$ ____

---

4. Make a garden that is 5×6 or 6×5.
Draw one bean in each square.
How many beans are there?

5×6 or

$6 \times 5 =$ ____

Name ______________________

Remembering

1. How many beans are planted in this garden?

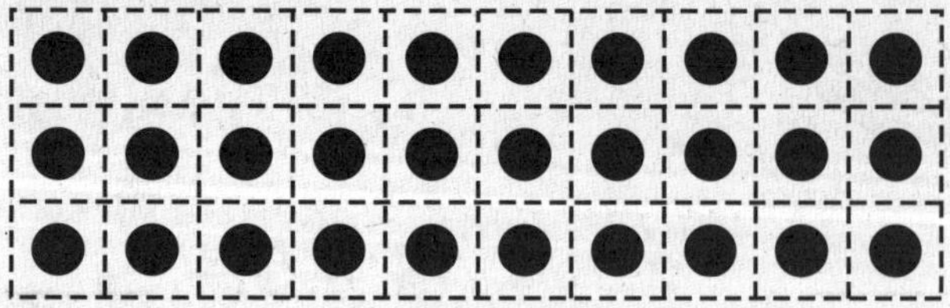

_____ × _____ or

_____ × _____ = _____

2. Complete the money table:

68¢			
Q		=	_____ ¢
D	3	=	_____ ¢
N		=	_____ ¢
P	3	=	_____ 3¢
			_____ ¢

3. Write 8 equations for the Math Mountain.

732

249 483

_____________ _____________

_____________ _____________

_____________ _____________

_____________ _____________

Solve the story problems.

4. The boys collected 542 coats, and the girls collected 368 coats for the clothing drive. How many more coats did the boys collect than the girls?

☐ _____________
label

5. Mr. Jones has 236 melons to sell at the fair. He has already sold 129. How many more melons does he have to sell?

☐ _____________
label

Name ____________________

Homework

1. How many apple trees are in this orchard? Write the 4s count-bys and the total.

_____ × _____ or

_____ × _____ = _____

_____ _____ _____ _____ _____ _____ _____

2. Make an array of 32 trees. Write the multiplication.

_____ × _____ or

_____ × _____ = _____

7–5 Name ____________________

Targeted Practice

Solve the problems. Write the count-bys and the total.

1. Leaves on a clover

_____ _____ _____ _____ _____ _____ _____ _____ _____

9 × 3 = _____

2. How many strawberries are in this carton?
Write the 4s count-bys and the total.

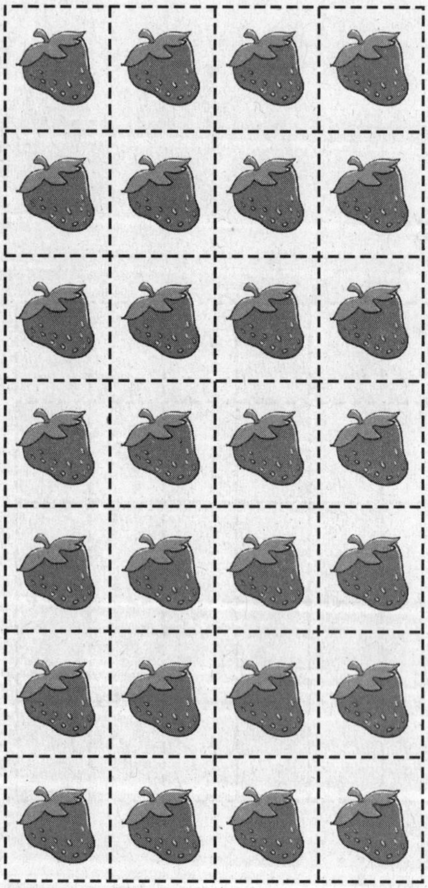

_____ × _____ or

_____ × _____ = _____

_____ _____ _____ _____ _____ _____ _____

Name ______________________

Homework

Draw in your answers. Write the numbers too.

1. Valeria has **twice** as many crackers as Brian.

Valeria has ________.

Brian has ________.

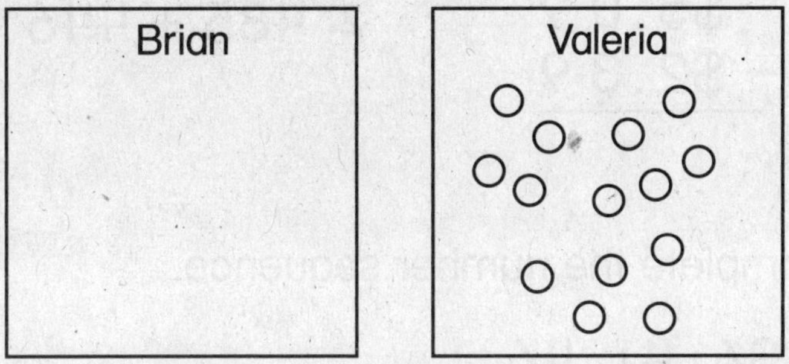

2. Our school has **double** the number of teachers as Grant School.

Our school has ________.

Grant has ________.

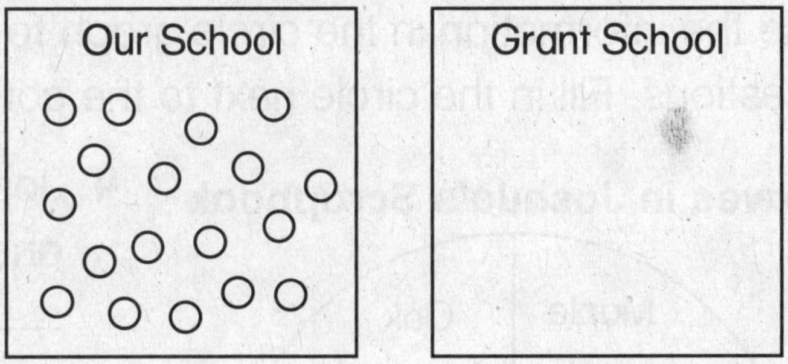

3. Fluffy and Muffy have **equal shares** of dog treats.

Fluffy has ________.

Muffy has ________.

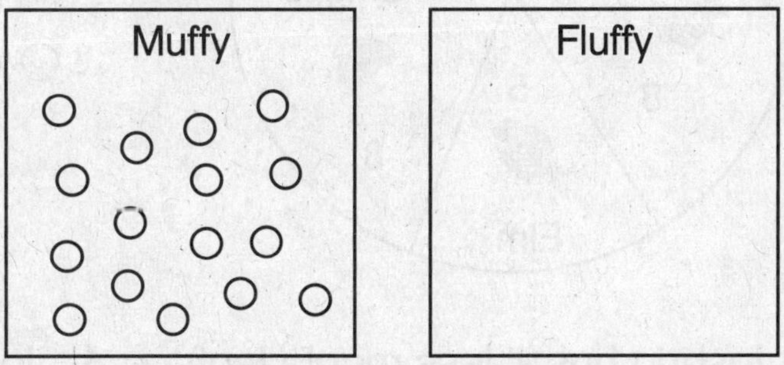

4. Main Street has **half** as many stoplights as First Street.

Main Street has ________.

First Street has ________.

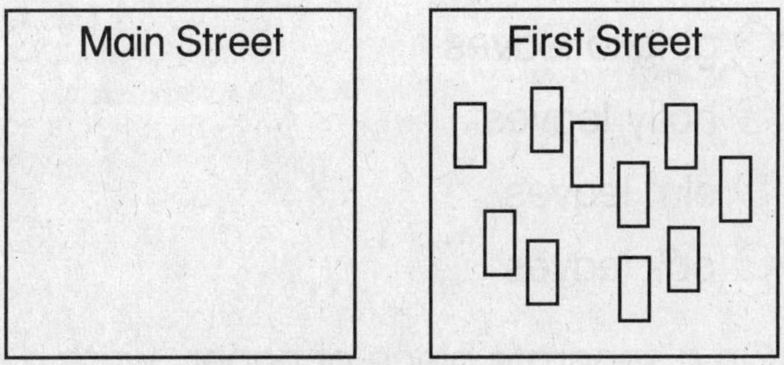

Name ______

Remembering

Add or subtract.

1. $5.09 − $2.39

2. 485 + 446 = ______

Complete the number sequence.

3. 36, 41, 46 ______, ______, ______, ______, ______ Rule: *n* ______

Use the information in the circle graph to answer the questions. Fill in the circle next to the correct answer.

Leaves in Joshua's Scrapbook

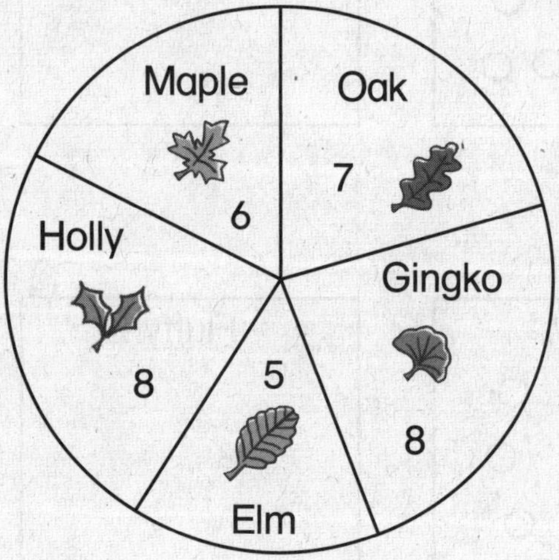

4. Joshua has the same amount of gingko and elm leaves as ______ and ______.
   - ○ maple and oak leaves
   - ○ holly and maple leaves
   - ○ elm and oak leaves
   - ○ gingko and maple leaves

5. Joshua has 1 less maple leaf than ______.
   - ○ gingko leaves
   - ○ holly leaves
   - ○ elm leaves
   - ○ oak leaves

6. Joshua has 3 more holly leaves than ______.
   - ○ oak leaves
   - ○ elm leaves
   - ○ maple leaves
   - ○ gingko leaves

7. On a separate piece of paper, write a story problem that takes two steps to solve. Then solve it.

Name ______________________

Homework

Does the figure have a line of symmetry? Write *yes* or *no.* If yes, draw one line of symmetry.

1. 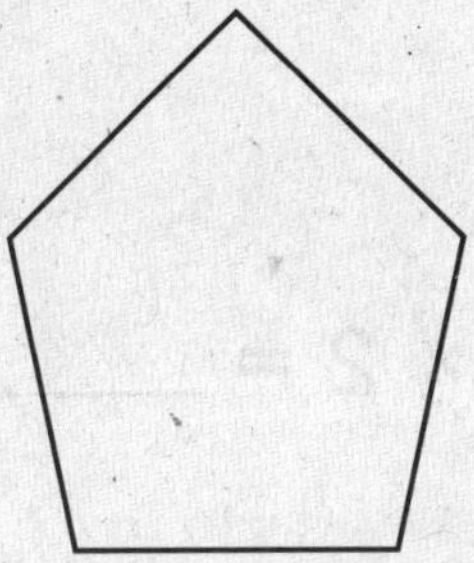

______

2. 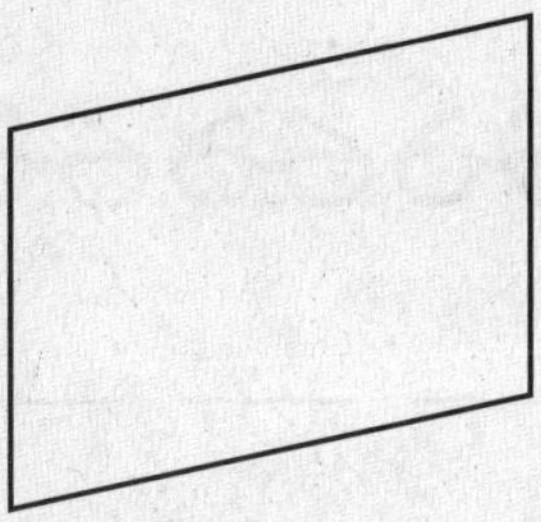

______

3. 

______

4. 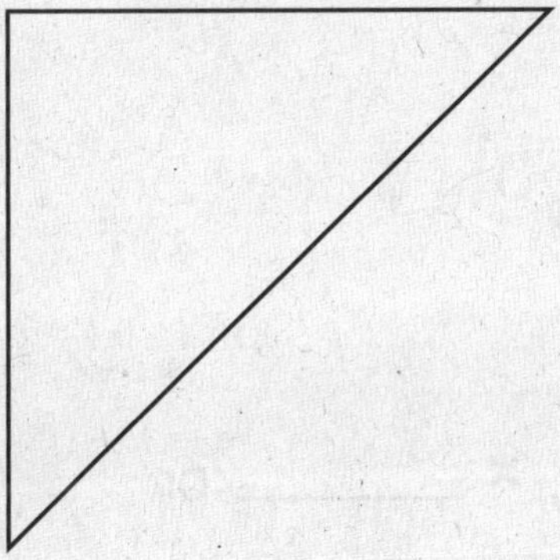

______

5. 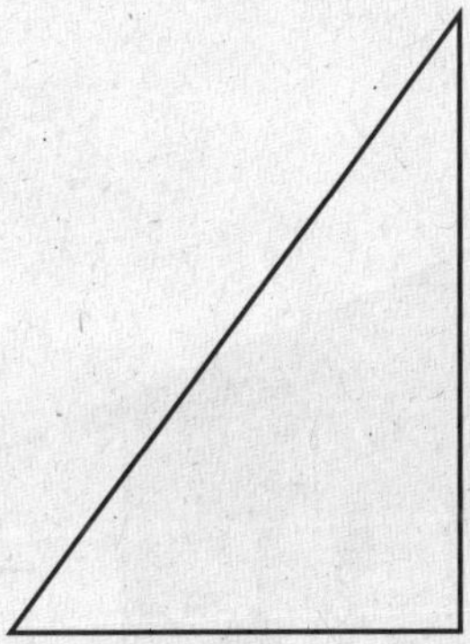

______

6. 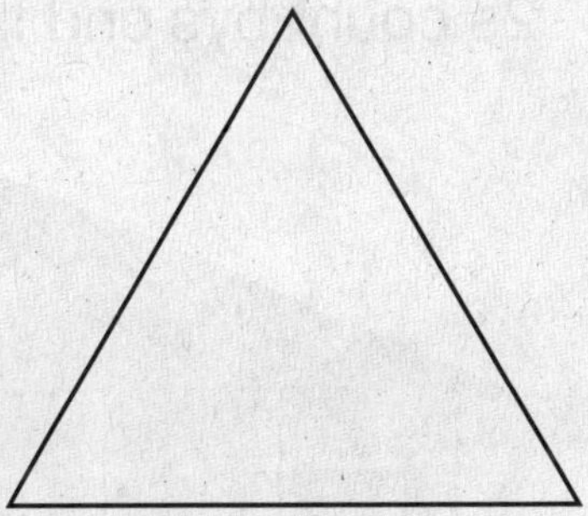

______

7. 

______

8. 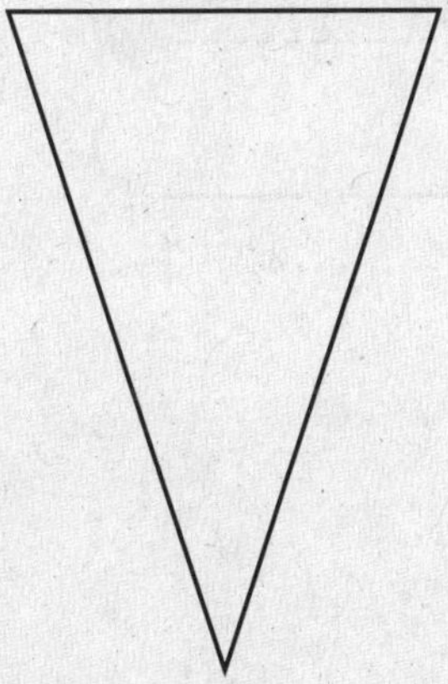

______

9. 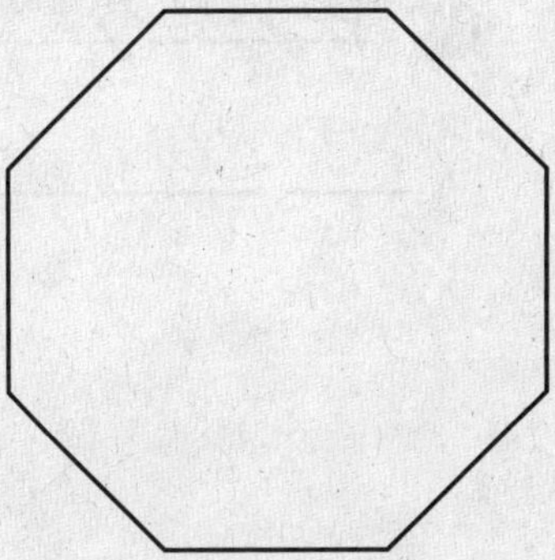

______

 Name ____________________

Targeted Practice

Solve the problems.

1. How many lenses are there? Write the count-bys and the total.

____ ____ ____ ____ ____ ____ ____ 7 × 2 = ______

2. How many chickens are in this barn? Write the 2s count-bys and the total.

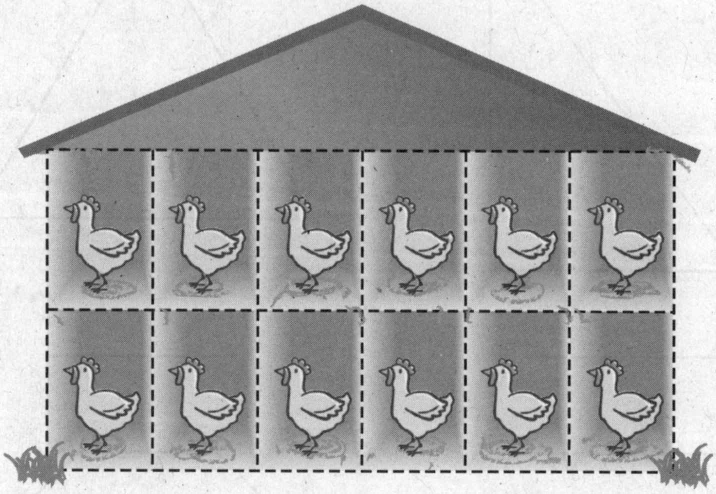

______ × ______ or

______ × ______ = ______

____ ____ ____ ____ ____ ____

 Name ______________________________

Homework

1. Shade in the fractions for the shapes.

$$\frac{1}{2}$$

$$\frac{2}{3} = \frac{1}{3} + \frac{1}{3}$$

$$\frac{3}{4} = \frac{1}{4} + \frac{1}{4} + \frac{1}{4}$$

2. How much is shaded? Write the fraction.

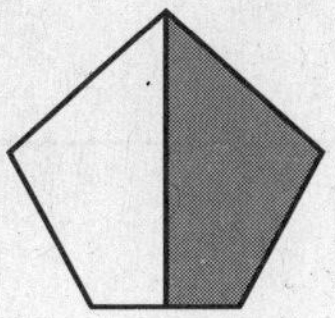 ______

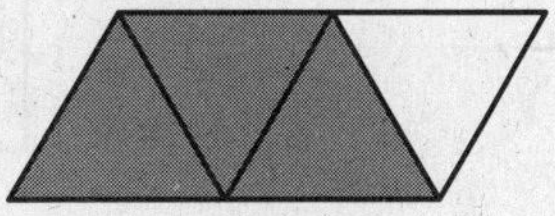 ______

Name ______________________

Remembering

Is the figure symmetrical? Write *yes* or *no*.
If yes, draw one line of symmetry.

1.

______

2.

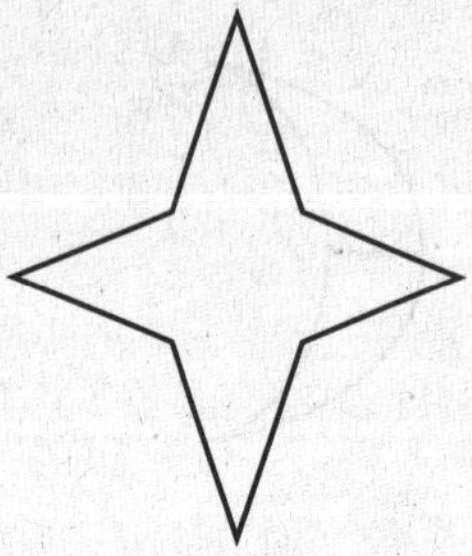

______

3.

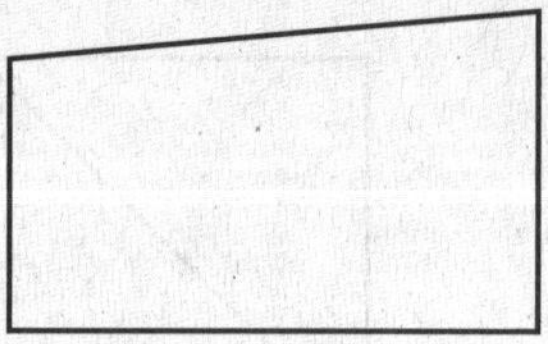

______

Add or subtract.

4.

$$\begin{array}{r} \$7.21 \\ -\ \$4.23 \\ \hline \end{array}$$

5.

$$\begin{array}{r} 479 \\ +\ 386 \\ \hline \end{array}$$

Draw in your answers. Write the numbers.

6. Sara has **double** the number of balloons as Ray.

Sara has ______.

Ray has ______.

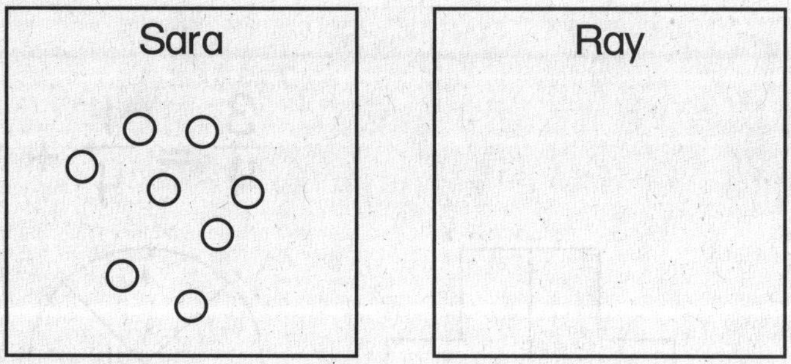

7. Luke has **half** as many chips as Leda.

Luke has ______.

Leda has ______.

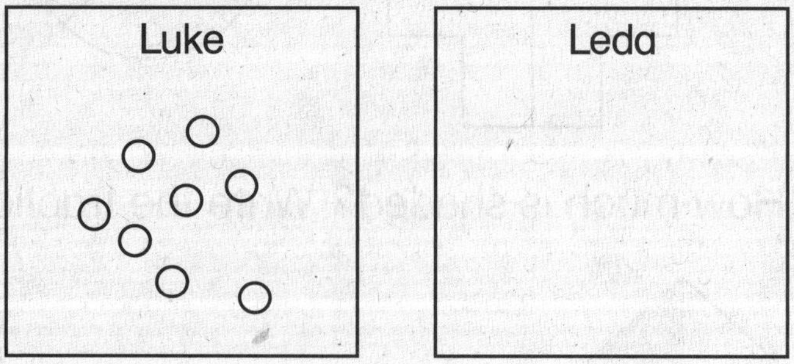

7–9

Name ______________________

Homework

Compare the shaded parts. Write >, <, or =.

1.

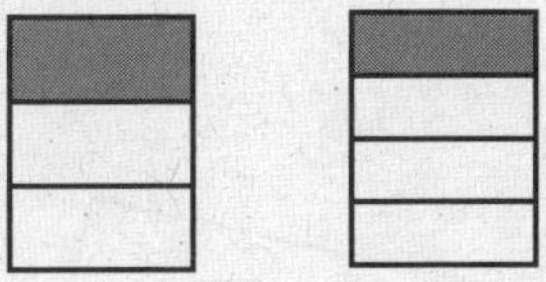

$\frac{1}{3}$ ◯ $\frac{1}{4}$

2.

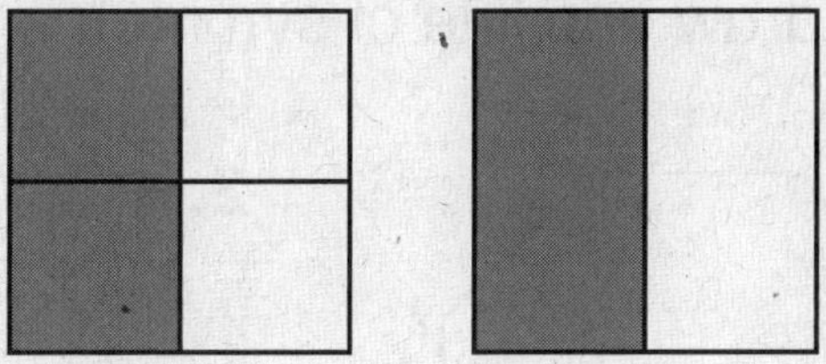

$\frac{2}{4}$ ◯ $\frac{1}{2}$

3.

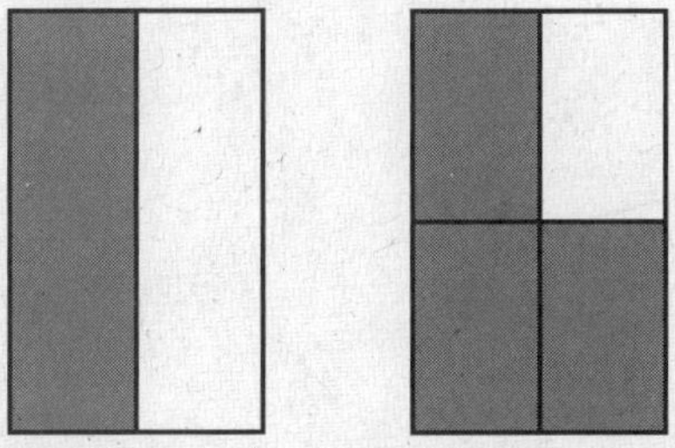

$\frac{1}{2}$ ◯ $\frac{3}{4}$

4.

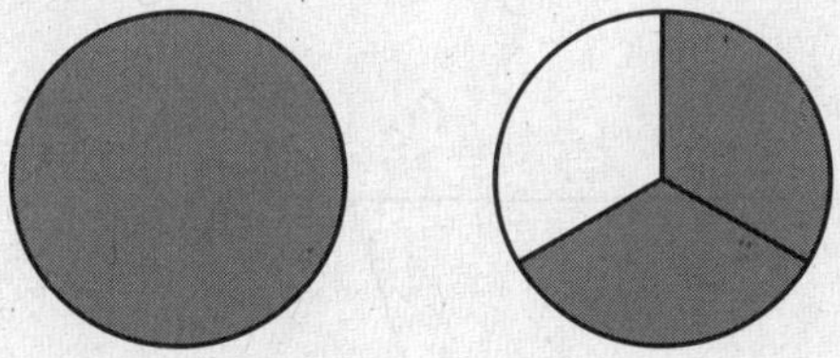

1 ◯ $\frac{2}{3}$

Complete the chart.

	Money Amount	Number of Cents	Dollars and Cents	Fraction of a Dollar
5.	5 dimes	________¢	\$0.50	$\frac{5}{10}$
6.	2 dimes	20¢	\$0.______	$\frac{\quad}{10}$
7.	42 pennies	________¢	\$0.42	$\frac{\quad}{100}$
8.	3 pennies	3¢	\$____.______	$\frac{\quad}{100}$

Name ____________________

Targeted Practice

Is the figure symmetrical? Write *yes* or *no*.
If yes, draw one line of symmetry.

1.
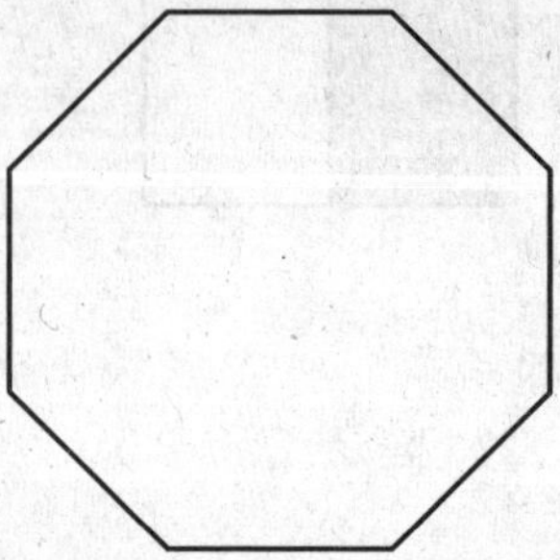
____

2.
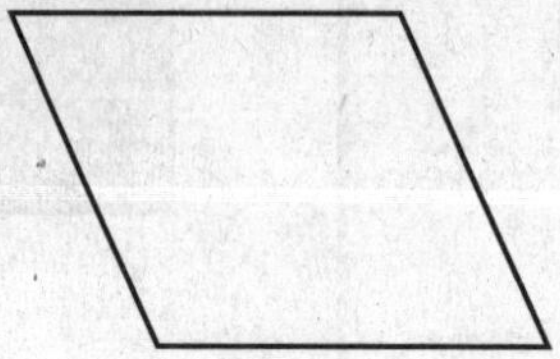
____

3.
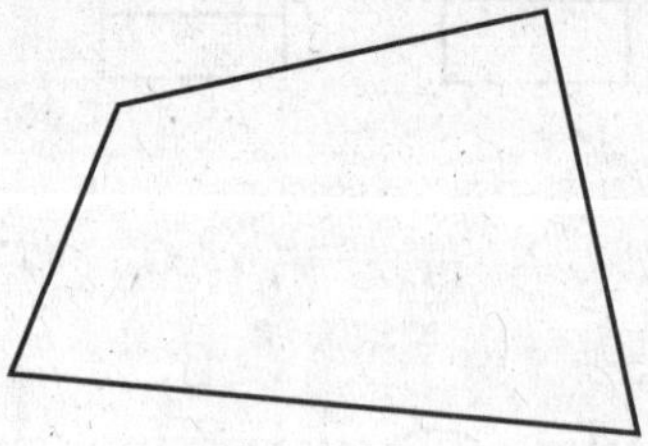
____

4.

____

5.
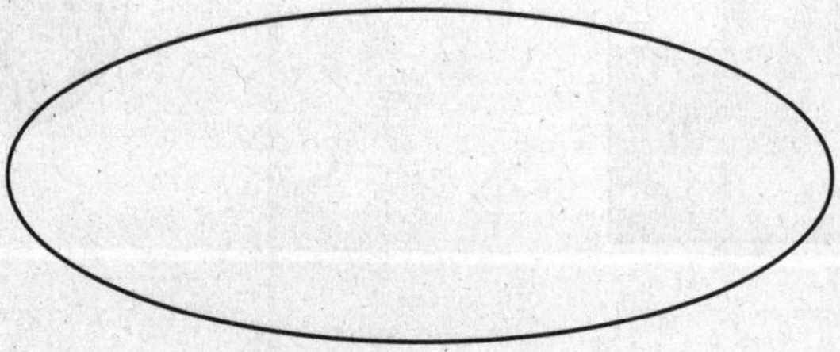
____

6.
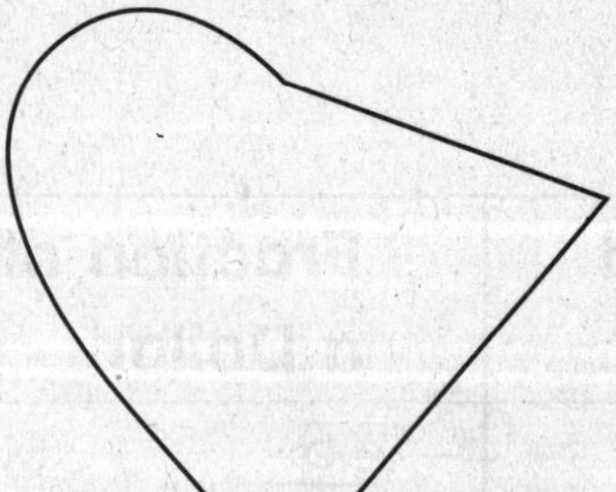
____

7.
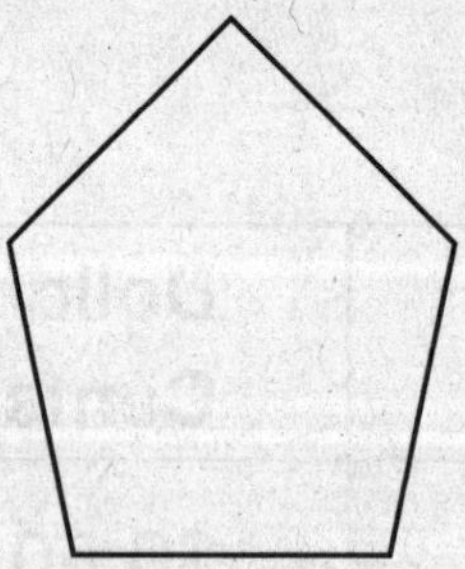
____

8.
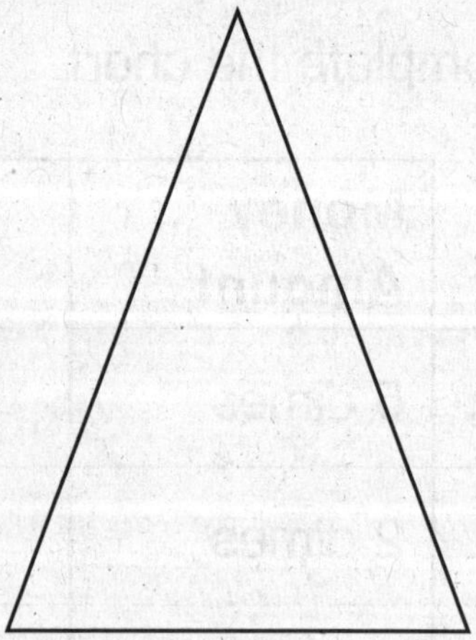
____

7-10

Homework

Name ______________________________

Look at the bag of cubes. Circle the correct event.

1. Which event is certain?

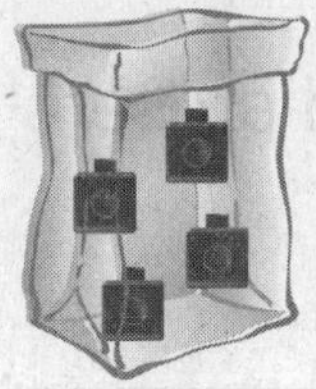

I will pick a black cube.

I will pick a white cube.

2. Which event is impossible?

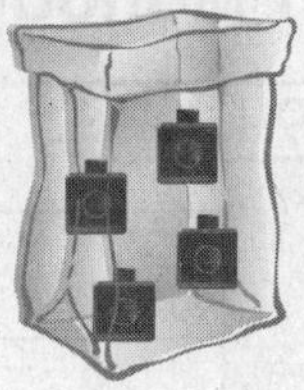

I will pick a black cube.

I will pick a white cube.

Look at the bag of cubes. How likely are you to pick a  than a 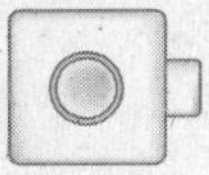 ?

3.

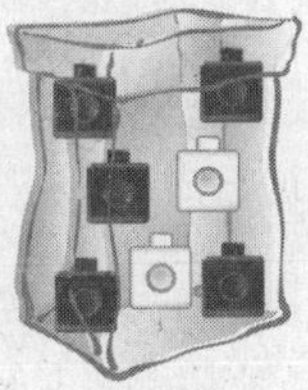

more likely

less likely

4.

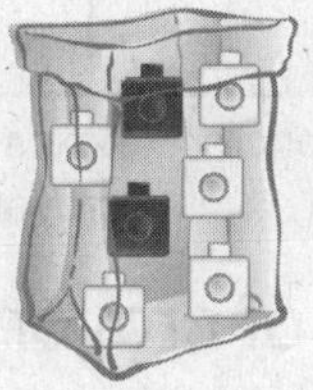

more likely

less likely

Color in the spinners to make the statements true.

5. This is a fair spinner.

6. This is an unfair spinner.

Name ____________________

Remembering

Use the information in the bar graph to answer the questions.

School Supplies Sold on Monday

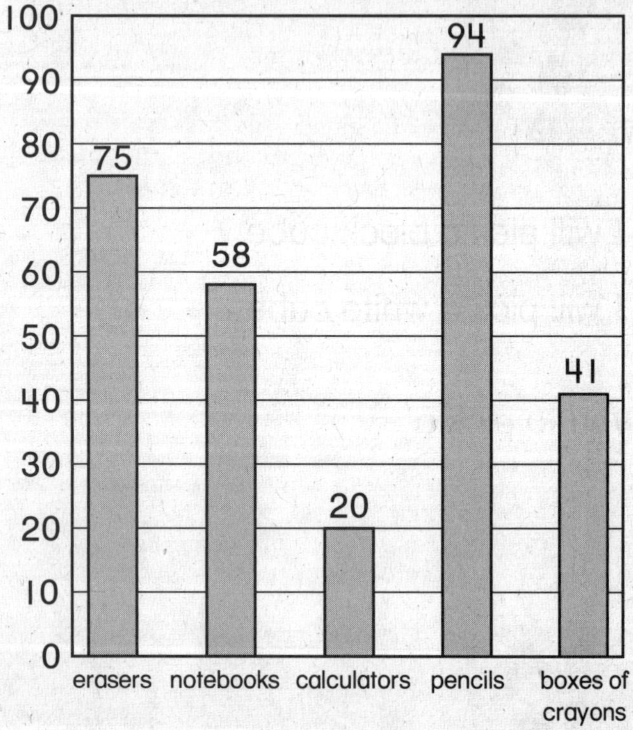

1. How many pencils and erasers were sold altogether?

____

2. How many fewer notebooks were sold than erasers?

____

3. How many more boxes of crayons were sold than calculators?

____

4. How many fewer pencils need to be sold to equal the number of notebooks sold?

____

Subtract.

5. $\begin{array}{r} 584 \\ -\ 275 \\ \hline \end{array}$

6. $\begin{array}{r} 427 \\ -\ 136 \\ \hline \end{array}$

7. $\begin{array}{r} 912 \\ -\ 458 \\ \hline \end{array}$

8. $\begin{array}{r} 203 \\ -\ 171 \\ \hline \end{array}$

9. Time On a separate piece of paper, draw what you do at 12 o'clock P.M. Show the time on a digital clock.

Name

Homework

Make an organized list to solve the problems.

Show your work.

1. Eli has a blue shirt and a tan shirt. He also has a pair of black pants and a pair of brown pants. How many different combinations of a shirt and pants can he wear?

☐ different combinations

Shirt Color		Pants Color
blue	→	black
blue	→	
tan	→	

2. Mr. Alvarez has lilies, roses, and tulips to put in a tall vase and in a short vase. How many different combinations can he arrange with the flowers and vases?

☐ different combinations

Flower		Vase
lilies	→	tall
lilies	→	
roses	→	

3. Blair packed a pair of boots and a pair of running shoes. She also packed a baseball cap, a sun hat, and a western hat. How many different combinations of shoes and hats can she wear?

☐ different combinations

Shoe	Hat

Name ______________________________

Targeted Practice

1. Shade in the fractions for the shapes.

$$\frac{2}{3} = \frac{1}{3} + \frac{1}{3}$$

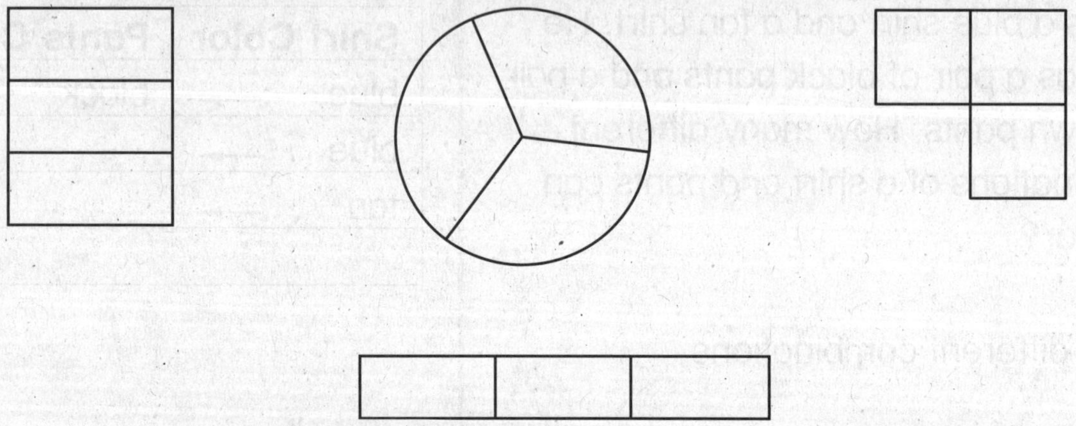

$$\frac{3}{4} = \frac{1}{4} + \frac{1}{4} + \frac{1}{4}$$

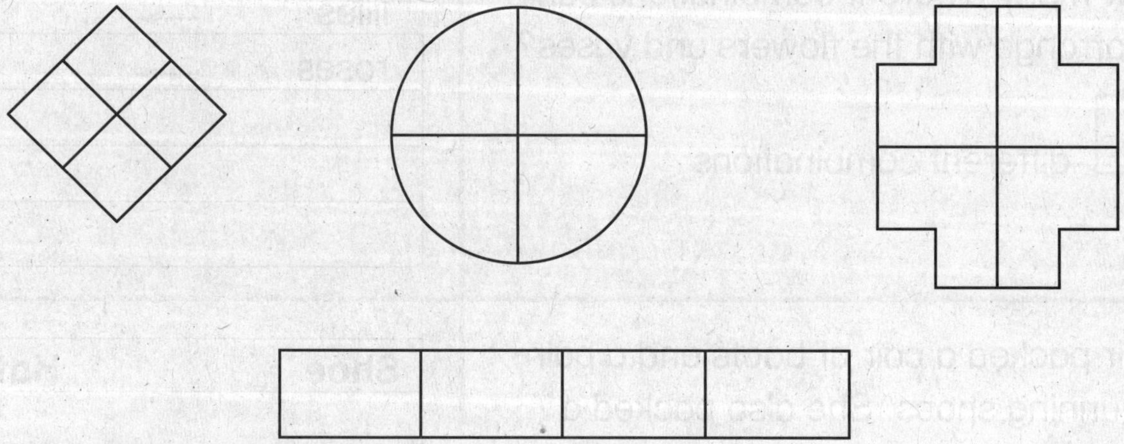

2. How much is shaded? Write the fraction.

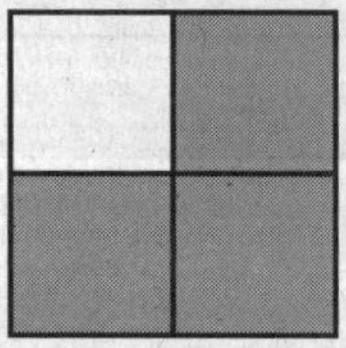 ______

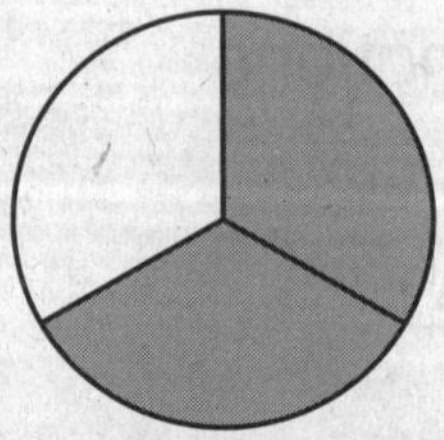 ______

G–1

Name ____________________

Homework

1. Use the width of your hand to measure the length of three objects. Measure the same objects using the width of a finger.

Object	Length (hands)	Length (fingers)

2. Find three containers. Use small objects, like beans or cups of rice or water, to measure the capacity of each container. Remember to include units in your answers.

Container	Capacity

3. Find three objects that are about the same size. Hold the objects one at a time to compare their masses. List the objects in order from least to greatest mass.

____

____

____

4. **On the Back** Describe how measuring length and capacity are similar.

Name ______________________

G–2

Name ______________________________

Homework

1. Find five objects at home to measure in inches. Estimate and measure the length of each object. If necessary, round the measurements. Complete the table.

Object	Estimated length (in.)	Measured length (in.)

2. Find five objects at home to measure in feet or yards. Complete the table. Remember to include units with your measurements.

Object	Measured length

3. Fill in the correct number.

1 ft = ______ in. 3 ft = ______ yd 1 yd = ______ in.

2 yd = ______ ft 3 ft = ______ in. 36 in. = ______ ft

4. On the Back Measure your height in feet. Measure the length of your leg and the length of your arm in inches. Make a drawing of yourself. Write the measurements on your drawing.

Name ______________________________